EATING IN

EATING IN

SUE LAWRENCE

hachette
SCOTLAND

First published in 2011 by
HACHETTE SCOTLAND,
an imprint of Hachette UK

1

Cataloguing in Publication Data is available from the British Library

ISBN: 978 0 7553 6005 5

Designed by Freight
Food styling by Maxine Clark
Photographs © Alan Donaldson
Printed and bound in China by Imago

Hachette Scotland's policy is to use papers that are natural, renewable and recyclable products and made from wood grown in sustainable forests. The logging and manufacturing processes are expected to conform to the environmental regulations of the country of origin.

HACHETTE SCOTLAND
An Hachette UK Company
338 Euston Road
London NW1 3BH

www.hachettescotland.co.uk
www.hachette.co.uk

Contents

To Pat, Euan, Faith and Jessica,
for always scraping their plates clean.

THANKS
Anna and Bob Anderson
Richard Barclay
Hilary Blackford
Lynda Boyle
Mary-An Charnley
Sheila and Marco Dafereras
Elisabeth and Jackie Hadden
Sue Hadden
Isabel and Martin Johnson
Hilary Lawrence
Pippa Lekner
Aggie MacKenzie
Fiona MacKinnes
Iain MacLeod
Jo MacSween
Claire McKay
Judi Matheson
Isabelle Plews
Carol Tollerton
Beverley Tricker

A SPECIAL MENTION TO:
Jenny Brown, my wonderful agent; Bob McDevitt, publisher
extraordinaire; Maxine Clark for her gorgeous food styling;
Alan Donaldson for his beautiful food photos; and Jo Roberts-Miller
and Jo Whitford for editing so brilliantly and patiently.
Thanks also to Linda Dick for her evocative landscape photos and to
Sejin Moon (www.sejinmoon.com) for her fabulous family photo.

Introduction

THESE DAYS BOTH family meals and entertaining are far more relaxed. Gone are the days when you'd have to spend ages polishing the silver, shining up the crystal glasses, soaking the oasis for the flower arrangements and starching the napkins. The tyranny of the hostess trolley is gone forever! Well, it certainly is in my house...

And whether it's just a midweek family supper or a casual Sunday lunch for friends, the emphasis is on informality. Things are laid-back, as befits a far more easy-going generation; and as befits a generation that is frantically busy most of the time and who like to relax with simple fare at a simple table, even when entertaining.

In *Eating In* the emphasis is also on another trend – that of cooking from local ingredients as often as possible. Also, there are no reduced, French-style sauces that take years of skill to perfect and hours to prepare, and no blowtorches or cheffy techniques here. You'll just find straightforward recipes that are both modern and yet somehow linked to the past. As a Scot, I like to create modern twists on the Scottish classics, such as *Partan Bree Risotto* or *Cullen Skink Pie*, bringing an old dish right into the 21st century, whilst still giving a reverential nod to the traditional recipe.

This book is not only for meals taken in the home but you'll find inspiration for dishes to eat in the great outdoors – picnics, barbecues, weekends away – and most seasonal festivities are covered, from Burns Night and Easter to Hallowe'en and Hogmanay. And not all of the recipes suggested for eating at home are for eating at a table – you'll find TV dinners, finger foods and buffet platters for parties.

Hopefully you'll come to agree that this easy, informal style is what food is all about these days. It's certainly how I see *Eating In*.

Chapter 1

Hogmanay Buffet

DOES THE PROSPECT of cooking for a crowd fill you with dread? Do you invariably resort to your trusty, old-favourite recipes when the guests number more than three or four? Of course, there's nothing wrong with sticking to a winning formula, but just occasionally it's good to try something a little different.

Over the festive season there is plenty of time to invite family and friends around for a casual buffet lunch or supper. A buffet is the easiest and most relaxed method of entertaining: once the food is on the table, you – the cook – can sit down with your guests and catch up on all the news. It also means there is no last-minute flapping over the stove – you, too, can enjoy all that delicious food at your leisure. Hogmanay is the ideal time to provide an ongoing buffet as people pop in and out... no doubt till the wee small hours!

Hogmanay is big news in Scotland. In fact it was only relatively recently that it took second place to Christmas as *the* festive celebration. I remember my father worked on Christmas Day up until the 1960s but had several days off over New Year. When I had my first job in 1980, I had only one day off for Christmas but about three days for Hogmanay. The festivities started on the 31 December and continued well into January. We Scots might have a reputation for being mean with money, but we are certainly not mean with our celebrations!

Over the New Year period, everyone goes 'first-footing' – visiting friends, neighbours and family members, from mischievous cousins to redoubtable great-aunts, to wish them happy New Year. It was considered lucky if the first person to cross the threshold after midnight was tall, dark and – you guessed it – handsome; and he had to carry a piece of black coal. The New Year was always toasted with a drink – traditionally a dram for the men, a sherry for the ladies and (yuk, I still remember it well) ginger 'wine' for the children. The traditional food was shortbread served with chunks of Cheddar cheese (try my recipe on page 106), sultana cake (see page 131) and black bun (a rich fruit cake enclosed in shortcrust pastry).

These days, there is still plenty of first-footing and Hogmanay parties, but there is also (hallelujah!) far more emphasis on food. Many friends now organise dinner or buffet parties, or go out to favourite restaurants; but they must be back home before midnight, to 'bring in the New Year' at their own hearth.

Here are some recipes you might want to add to your repertoire of festive dishes – they have the advantage of being served cold or at room temperature so they will be ready no matter what time your visitors arrive. If you would prefer a hot dish, try *Lynda's Beef and Porcini Casserole* on page 178.

Chinese noodle salad with mango, crab and ginger

SERVES 8

2 × 250g packets dried egg noodles

500g / 1 lb 2 oz white crabmeat

6 large spring onions, chopped

3 heaped tablespoons freshly chopped coriander

2 large mangoes, peeled and diced

1 large papaya, peeled and diced

250g / 9 oz large prawns, cooked and shelled

FOR THE DRESSING

1 heaped tablespoon freshly grated root ginger

150ml / 5 fl oz sunflower oil

2 tablespoons freshly squeezed lime juice

1 tablespoon Thai fish sauce

several shakes of Tabasco (or another hot chilli sauce)

THIS IS IDEAL for a buffet table, as it can be made up to six hours in advance, kept in the refrigerator and simply tossed well before serving.

First make the dressing by shaking everything together in a screw-top jar. Taste and add more Tabasco if you like it hot. Season with salt and pepper.

Cook the noodles according to the packet instructions, then drain well and toss in all the dressing while still warm. Allow to cool then add the crab, spring onions, coriander, mangoes and papaya. Toss again gently to mix evenly. (At this stage it can be covered and chilled for up to six hours.)

Just before serving, toss again, pile in a mound on a serving plate, and garnish with the prawns.

Turkey tonnato

leftover turkey meat (approx ⅓ turkey),
or the meat from 1 cooked chicken, sliced

1 × 400g jar of quality mayonnaise

2 × 200g tins of tuna, drained

1 × 50g tin anchovies, drained

50ml / 2 fl oz dry white wine

splash of lemon juice (optional)

2 tablespoons of capers or caper berries, to decorate

THE CLASSIC TONNATO of northern Italy is usually prepared with veal, but the sauce – a tuna mayonnaise – also works beautifully with cold turkey or chicken. It can be served as part of a cold buffet or with green salad and Italian bread. This is another dish that can be made in advance and kept covered in the fridge until needed.

Lay the sliced turkey on to a serving plate.

Place the mayonnaise, tuna and half of the anchovies in a food processor with the wine. Process until well combined, then taste and season with salt and pepper, if required. (You might also want to add a little lemon juice.)

Spoon the tuna mayonnaise over the turkey slices.

Cut the remaining anchovies in half lengthways and place them crossways – lattice-style – on top of the tuna. Dot each square with a couple of capers and serve at room temperature.

Warm chocolate, shortbread and pistachio mousse cake

SERVES 8–10

350g / 12 oz dark chocolate (minimum 60% cocoa solids)

200g / 7 oz butter

3 large free-range eggs

300g / 10½ oz golden caster sugar

150g / 5½ oz shortbread, broken up into bite-size chunks (not crumbs)

100g / 3½ oz pistachio kernels, shelled (not salted)

THIS IS AN ideal pudding on Hogmanay in Scotland, since most houses will have a plethora of shortbread around this time. It is light, gooey and simply wonderful when freshly baked. The texture becomes more dense the day after it is made but the cake will still taste divine served with a dollop of crème fraîche.

~

Preheat the oven to 170°C / 325°F / Gas 3 and butter and line a 23cm / 9 in spring-form cake tin.

Melt the chocolate and butter together; I do this in the microwave, though you can also do it in a saucepan over a gentle heat.

Beat the eggs and sugar together until thick and pale (4–5 minutes in a food mixer; 8–10 minutes by hand).

Fold the egg mixture into the chocolate, and then gently stir in the shortbread and nuts. Tip into the prepared cake tin.

Bake for about 40 minutes, until still a little wobbly in the middle. Remove to a wire rack and leave for an hour.

Remove the sides of the tin and serve in wedges while it is barely warm, or at room temperature, with drizzled pouring cream or crème fraîche and berries.

Chapter 2

New Year's Day Lunch

AS A CHILD, my memories of Ne'er Day – as New Year's Day is traditionally known in Scotland – involved a car journey to Dundee to visit and first-foot both sets of grandparents and a full set of aunts, uncles and cousins. Many of these journeys seemed to involve snow for, although I can only remember one genuine white Christmas as a child, New Year was often not only bitterly cold but snowy, or at least very frosty.

At each house we were proffered food and drink and it would have been rude to refuse any. I remember at my great-auntie Maggie's flat, up three flights of tenement stairs, there was blackcurrant cordial, 'shortie' and of course whisky. There would be savoury titbits on offer elsewhere.

The New Year's Day meal was the same over much of Scotland and certainly in Dundee: steak pie (a delicious meaty, gravy-enriched stew with a pastry topping, similar to my recipe on page 73) served with mashed potatoes and either a green vegetable such as cabbage or (more likely in Dundee) some other 'vegetable' such as butter beans.

Although the slant on Hogmanay has changed a little over the years, with food being given slightly more emphasis (more and more people going out to dinner first), New Year's Day has remained pretty much unchanged, with delicious food that is easy to prepare in advance (still often steak pie). After all, there will still be sore heads, even following a food-filled Hogmanay!

Once the New Year's Day meal is over, the first-footing continues over the following day or two. And, with the street parties that take place in all major Scottish cities these days, Ne'er Day is still a time for families to get together and celebrate in the time-honoured manner, with tradition very much to the fore.

I've given a couple of recipe ideas here for late (it's always late!) Ne'er Day lunch. The salmon tart can be served warm or cold with salad, and the stovies are classic Scottish comfort food to be served alone – nothing else is needed apart from a big appetite.

Hot smoked salmon tart with rocket and crème fraîche

SERVES 4–6

3 tablespoons freshly grated Parmesan

300g / 10½ oz hot-smoked salmon, flaked

50g / 1¾ oz rocket, roughly chopped

3 large free-range eggs

the zest of 1 lemon

200ml / 7 fl oz crème fraîche

FOR THE PASTRY

200g / 7 oz plain flour, sifted

125g / 4½ oz unsalted butter, diced

1 large free-range egg, beaten

Hot-smoked salmon

During a visit to the Outer Hebrides, we had Salar hot-smoked salmon in many guises – with scrambled eggs at breakfast, in salads as starters and in sandwiches at lunch. I visited their smoke-house near Lochcarron on South Uist to see the production. The salmon comes from Loch Duart and is then cleaned, filleted and dry-salted. The salt is then rinsed off and the fish is hot-smoked over oak chips until it is moist and flaky. They leave the skin on their salmon so it does not dis-integrate. It is hugely versatile as it can also be tossed into pastas, risottos, tarts or be used as a topping for soups.

THIS CAN BE made in advance and frozen, or you can freeze the uncooked pastry case then bake it fresh on the day.

~

To make the pastry, place the flour and butter in a food processor with a pinch of salt. Process briefly then, with the machine running, add the egg. Finally, bring the dough together with your hands, cover with clingfilm and chill for half an hour or so.

Roll out to fit a 25cm/10 in tart tin, prick all over and chill well again – preferably overnight.

Preheat the oven to 190°C / 375°F / Gas 5.

Fill the pastry-lined tart tin with foil and baking beans and bake blind for 15 minutes. Remove the foil and cook for a further 5-10 minutes until just cooked.

Remove from the oven and sprinkle the Parmesan over the base while it is still hot, and then leave to cool.

Scatter the salmon over the base and then top with the rocket, pressing down a little.

Stir the eggs, lemon zest and crème fraîche together, seasoning with salt and pepper, and then pour slowly over the salmon and rocket.

Bake for 30–40 minutes until set and tinged with golden brown. Serve warm or cold with salad.

Goose fat stovies

SERVES 6–8

3 tablespoons goose fat

2 onions, peeled and sliced

3 large potatoes, peeled and thinly sliced
(I do this in my food processor)

2–3 tablespoons meat jelly
(or beef stock)

EVERYONE SEEMS TO have a tin of goose fat at Christmas to roast their potatoes in with the turkey these days. So what to do with the remaining fat in the tin? Stovies, of course! Usually made with dripping, this version is a revelation – they are sublime. Stovies are ideal served as a casual family meal at any time on New Year's Day.

~

Melt the fat in a heavy-based saucepan and fry the onions for 10–15 minutes until golden.

Add the potato slices and turn carefully in the fat: be careful not to break them up. Season well with salt and pepper.

Add the meat jelly (or stock) and heat until melted. Cover tightly and cook over a low heat for 30–40 minutes, or until the potatoes are tender and have absorbed all the liquid. (Add a splash of hot water if they seem too dry.) While they are cooking, shake the pan often (holding onto the lid) to prevent sticking; do not stir or you will break up the delicate potato slices. Serve piping hot.

Stovies

This is a delicious dish of onions and potatoes that are cooked in dripping (the white fat on the surface of the meat jelly after pouring off the meat juices from your roasting tin and chilling) and then cooked slowly in meat jelly – or stock – until tender.

When my parents were growing up in Dundee stovies were regular fare, either as a complete dish or with sausages. Special dripping would be bought from the butcher's, as ordinary Dundonians seldom had roast meat.

According to F. Marian McNeill, the word stovies (stoved potatoes) comes from the French 'étuver', which means to stew or to dry in a stove

– one of the many Auld Alliance words that continue to flourish in Scottish kitchens. Stovies are also very similar to Pan Haggerty, a dish from the north-east of England consisting of sliced onions and sliced potatoes cooked in dripping in a deep skillet, which is then covered with a lid and cooked slowly until tender. Just like stovies, it was traditionally served on Mondays after a Sunday Roast.

Stovies are now classic pub fare throughout Scotland: they are ideal for soaking up vast quantities (or small quantities – less common in Scotland, however) of alcohol. And, as you travel around Scotland, your stovies will vary. In Arbroath and Aberdeen, corned beef or chopped roast meat are often added, and they are served with oatcakes. In Orkney, pieces of brisket are stirred in. My favourite way to serve them is just as they are (they already have so much flavour from the dripping and meat jelly), with thick oatcakes and a glass of cold milk.

Lemon curd and bramble cream pie

SERVES 8

250g / 9 oz ginger biscuits, crushed

85g / 3 oz butter, melted

200g / 7 oz lemon curd
(preferably home-made)

1 × 250g tub mascarpone

1 × 300ml tub crème fraîche

500g / 1 lb 2 oz brambles (blackberries)

YES, I KNOW brambles (this is what we Scots call blackberries) are not in season in January but, apart from raspberries, they are the best fruit to freeze. And they defrost much better than raspberries. So, don't forget to save some of the stash when you buy brambles from the farmshop in the late summer or when you pick them yourselves in the early autumn, so you can make this delicious pie come the New Year.

To make the base, combine the biscuits and butter, and then press the mixture into the base of a 23cm / 9 in spring-form cake tin. Chill well.

Mix the lemon curd, mascarpone and crème fraîche together in a bowl and then pile this on top of the biscuits. Spread evenly and cover with the berries. Serve at room temperature.

Chapter 3

A Bowl of Soup

IT MIGHT HAVE been after a day of sledging down the street, all muffled up in woolly hats and gloves to keep out the winter chill, or a day of clambering over haystacks in the fields behind the garden, when even t-shirts and shorts were too hot in the summer sun, but our kitchen – and most kitchens in Scotland – would have a soup pot on the go, whatever the weather. Come rain, hail or shine, there it would stand, ready to be heated up and the contents ladled out.

For while a bowl of piping hot soup makes sense when there is a biting winter chill, it is also served in summer, even in those occasional Scottish heat waves, because that is what Scots tradition dictates. I remember being struck, during my year living in northern Finland, how seldom soup was served in that bitterly cold climate – only once a week on Thursdays, when thick pea soup was dished up in schools, army barracks or office canteens throughout the entire country. In Scotland, however, once a day is mandatory.

My octogenarian father only ever deviates from the daily soup routine if he is eating out. And, even then, you can see he is struggling to resist the good bowl of wholesome broth as starter, feeling obliged to order the bruschetta with rocket and buffalo mozzarella. Whether it is Scotch broth bulging with barley and vegetables, cock-a-leekie, with its characteristic prunes, or 'bawd bree' – a gutsy game soup made from hare – soup has always been the prelude to any meal.

My mother recalls broth being referred to simply as 'kail' (the Scots spelling of kale), since this is the main vegetable in that thick, nourishing soup. And the most commonly used piece of equipment in our kitchen was the soup pot, known as the kail pot in times past. The other was the girdle (or griddle) for the daily batches of scones, pancakes and bannocks. The iron kail pot and the iron girdle were the two most basic pieces of cooking equipment found in crofts and cottages over the centuries throughout Scotland.

And, although nowadays you might occasionally come across a thin soup or a consommé in a Scottish home, you will seldom find chilled soup, though I have included two recipes here that can be served cold if you prefer. We Scots believe that, by its very nature, soup must be piping hot, hearty and inviting, and served all through the year.

Pea and mint soup with hot-smoked salmon

SERVES 4

50g / 1¾ oz butter

1 large onion, peeled and chopped

approx 1.5kg / 3 lb 5oz pea pods, shelled
(or 500g / 1 lb 2 oz frozen peas)

3 heaped tablespoons fresh mint leaves

600ml/20 fl oz hot chicken or vegetable stock

hot-smoked salmon (such as Salar
from South Uist), to serve

THIS CAN BE served hot or cold and, though the soup is fine served on its own (perhaps with a garnish of mint leaf), it is even more fabulous topped with flakes of hot-smoked salmon.

———— ～ ————

Melt the butter in a saucepan and then add the onion. Gently sauté for about 10 minutes.

Stir in the fresh (or undefrosted frozen) peas with two tablespoons of the mint. Coat well in the fat and then add the hot stock. Bring back to the boil.

Reduce to a simmer and cook, covered, for 8–10 minutes until tender but still vivid green.

Tip into a liquidiser or blender with the remaining mint and purée (you may have to do this in two batches). Season well, according to taste, and then reheat gently before serving in warm bowls, topped with flakes of hot-smoked salmon. Otherwise, chill in the fridge after puréeing and serve cold.

Roasted tomato soup with goats' cheese

SERVES 3–4

1kg / 2 lb 4 oz vine-ripened tomatoes, halved

3 tablespoons extra virgin olive oil

3 fat garlic cloves, unpeeled

15g / ½ oz basil leaves, plus extra to garnish

1 tablespoon balsamic vinegar

FOR THE GOATS' CHEESE CREAM

50g / 1¾ oz soft goats' cheese

the juice of 1 small lemon

some olive oil

THIS EASY AND tasty soup can be served hot with some of the goats' cheese cream plopped on top or chilled and served with an olive oil ice cube floating in the middle. Despite tradition, some Scots are taking to cold soups!

To make the ice cube simply pour some extra virgin olive oil into an ice-cube tray (only enough to half fill each cube) and freeze (this takes a couple of hours). Then plop out and into the chilled soup.

⁓

Preheat the oven to 190°C / 375°F / Gas 5.

To make the goats' cheese cream, place in a small blender with the lemon juice and whizz with enough olive oil (roughly 3–4 tablespoons) to become a purée. Season to taste with salt and pepper.

Place the tomato halves, cut-side up, on a baking tray with the unpeeled garlic cloves. Drizzle over the oil and season with salt and pepper. Roast for about 45 minutes.

Snip the ends off the garlic cloves and squeeze the innards into a food processor, along with the rest of the contents of the baking tray. Add the basil and vinegar and blend until smooth, adding boiling water, if necessary (some tomatoes give out enough liquid). The consistency should be soup-like but thick.

Season generously to taste with salt and pepper, before either reheating to serve hot with some of the goat's cheese cream, or serving cold with an olive oil ice cube.

Smokie broccoli soup

SERVES 4

2 tablespoons olive oil

1 onion, peeled and chopped

300g / 10½ oz potatoes, peeled and chopped

approx 700g / 1 lb 9 oz broccoli, chopped

1 teaspoon mild curry powder

1 litre / 1¾ pints hot light chicken
or vegetable stock

1 Arbroath smokie, flaked

a handful of chives, snipped

THIS IS A really easy soup, rustled up in a flash, which looks impressive with its vivid green colour. A hearty bowl can be served as a meal in itself at lunchtime, or a dinky, little, canapé-sized portion in an espresso cup could work as an aperitif.

———— ∾ ————

Heat the oil in a large pan, and then gently fry the onion for a couple of minutes.

Add the potatoes, stir well and then add the broccoli.

Sprinkle over the curry powder and cook for about a minute, stirring well.

Pour in the hot stock and bring back to the boil. Season well, to taste, and then simmer, covered, for 10–15 minutes, or until the vegetables are tender.

Liquidise or blend until smooth (you may have to do this in two batches), and then serve topped with flakes of smokie and snipped chives.

Lentil and ginger soup served with naan bread

SERVES 6

25g / 1 oz butter

1 onion, peeled and chopped

2 carrots, peeled and chopped

3 garlic cloves, peeled and chopped

2 heaped teaspoons freshly grated root ginger

350g / 12 oz orange lentils, well-rinsed

1 bay leaf

1.4 litres / 2½ pints hot chicken or vegetable stock

a handful of fresh coriander leaves

naan bread, to serve

A TWIST ON classic Scottish fare: good old lentil soup. Add some ground cumin with the ginger for an added aromatic hit!

⁓

Heat the butter in a saucepan and add the onion, carrots, garlic and ginger. Cook gently for 10–15 minutes until softened, then add the lentils, bay leaf, hot stock and salt and pepper. Increase the heat, bring to the boil and cover. Lower the heat and simmer for about 30 minutes, then fish out the bay leaf and liquidise or blend until smooth. Taste for seasoning, adding salt and pepper accordingly. Serve piping hot with some coriander on top and warm naan bread on the side.

Parsley and Brazil nut soup

SERVES 4

25g / 1 oz butter

1 tablespoon olive oil

1 onion, peeled and chopped

2 sticks celery, chopped

500g / 1 lb 2 oz potatoes, peeled and chopped

1 large leek, washed and sliced

150g / 5½ oz fresh parsley (flat-leaf or curly), stalks and leaves, washed

850ml / 1½ pints hot light chicken or vegetable stock

4–6 large Brazil nuts, to serve

DURING A VISIT to Sao Paulo, I saw and ate many fabulous things. At the Mercado Municipal, possibly the best food market in the world, I saw the most amazing range of fruits, fish, cheese and fresh and cured meats. Once you have had your fill of gazing and tasting, you can go upstairs to a vast hall to eat *bolinho de bacalha* (salt cod fritters) or pies filled with chicken, cheese, palm hearts or shrimp. While I was there, I also ate at D.O.M., one of the country's finest restaurants. It serves a slant on northern Brazilian (Amazonian) foods, which means that Brazil nuts are very much on the menu. As well as a divine Brazil nut tart served with whisky ice-cream and a powdering of curry (I know!), I had the most delicious soup of greens, with shrimps as a garnish, on to which the waiter shaved some Brazil nuts. A triumph! I now like to serve Brazil nuts with my old-favourite herb soup, which uses both stalk and leaf of that old-favourite herb – parsley.

～

Heat the butter and oil in saucepan and then gently fry the onion, celery, potatoes and leek for 10 minutes.

Stir in the parsley (keeping some leaves aside) and pour in the hot stock. Add ½ teaspoon of salt and plenty of freshly ground black pepper, bring back to the boil, cover and simmer for 15–20 minutes, or until tender.

Tip into a liquidiser or blender with the reserved parsley leaves and process until smooth (you may have to do this in two batches) adding a splash of boiling water if too thick. Check the seasoning and reheat gently.

Serve piping hot in warm bowls and then, using a coarse grater or vegetable peeler (one you would shave Parmesan with), grate some Brazil nut over each bowl.

Chapter 4
Burns Supper and St Andrew's Night

PART OF SCOTTISH culture for many years, the ritual of Burns suppers was begun by friends of the poet Robert Burns after his death in 1796 as a tribute to his memory. Although the basic format of the evening has remained unchanged over the years (The Selkirk Grace, The Immortal Memory, The Toast to the Lassies, its Response and so on), the food has moved with the times, even while adhering more or less to the soup, haggis and pudding formula. As for the drink: obligatory whisky for all the toasts (of which there are many). Is it any wonder that it's far from a quiet night?

Haggis is the centre point of a Burns supper, not only because it is now revered as Scotland's national dish, but also because of Burns' poem 'To A Haggis'. During the third verse, the kilted reciter ceremoniously stabs the haggis and the euphoric guests gaze admiringly as its 'gushing entrails' are revealed. In the bard's own words:

And then, O what a glorious sight,
Warm-reekin', rich!

Meanwhile, St Andrew's Night is being celebrated more and more these days and, although there is less in the way of strict ceremony at these occasions, there is also a definite nod to traditional Scottish fare.

And, whether it's 25 January (Burns Night) or 30 November (St Andrew's Day), once the plates are cleared and the glasses have been refilled for the toasts, the accordions and fiddles begin to limber up for the ceilidh that will invariably last well into the wee small hours!

Hummus
with haggis
and pine nuts

SERVES 6–10

1 × 400g can chick peas, drained

2 garlic cloves, peeled and chopped

the juice of 2 lemons

2 tablespoons tahini paste

2 teaspoons ground cumin

2 tablespoons fresh coriander leaves

some extra virgin olive oil

½ haggis (meat or vegetarian)

50g / 1¾ oz pine nuts

pomegranate seeds, optional

THIS IS MY variation of a delicious Middle Eastern dish of hummus, topped with cumin-scented minced lamb. The pomegranate makes it more authentically Middle Eastern – and also makes it look more gorgeous!

— ∼ —

Place the first six ingredients in a food processor and process briefly before adding about 4 tablespoons of extra virgin olive oil. Process again until it is a thickish purée, and then loosen the mixture with 2–3 tablespoons of warm water. Season to taste and tip into a shallow bowl.

Heat the haggis until piping hot (I do this in the microwave by cutting it open and scooping the contents into a microwave bowl, covering it with clingfilm and cooking for few minutes, stirring often).

Dry-fry the pine nuts in a hot frying pan for a couple of minutes, shaking constantly, until toasted.

Spoon the hot haggis over the top of the hummus, scatter over the toasted pine nuts (and pomegranate seeds, if using them) and serve with warm flat bread or toasted pittas.

Haggis

Macsweens factory just outside Edinburgh is where most of the world's haggis is produced. The first stage in the production is when the lamb lobes (lights) – the lungs – are cooked for some three hours, before being mixed with cooked beef fat, medium and pinhead oatmeal, onions and the special seasoning which contains white pepper,

mace, salt and coriander. After it is all minced together the essential tasting begins. One of the Macsween family tastes and checks that the seasoning is correct. Then the mixture is filled into the natural casings, which are made of washed and salted ox bung or lamb's runner (intestine). They are then pricked and clipped at intervals, to allow for expansion, and cooked in the steam room for an hour or so before being cooled down overnight and vacuum-packed. Because they are already cooked they only require reheating once you get them home. Typically they are served with neeps and tatties – and probably a dram.

Scallops with haggis and pea mash

SERVES 4

12 plump fresh scallops

some olive oil

1kg/2 lb 4 oz floury potatoes, peeled and chopped

250g/9 oz peas (fresh or frozen)

100g/3½ oz butter, softened

½ haggis

DURING A TOUR of the Western Isles, we enjoyed many fabulous meals, one of which took place at the Polochar Inn, at the southern end of South Uist, a mere ten minutes away from the new causeway over to the pretty island of Eriskay. At Polochar we dined on locally landed scallops with haggis. And, although the more usual companion for scallops is black pudding, I find this is a very tasty alternative.

~

If the scallops are very thick, separate the white scallop muscle from the orange coral: the coral cooks more quickly and tends to burst if they are in a hot pan for too long. Otherwise, leave whole. Marinate in a little olive oil and set aside for at least 20 minutes.

Meanwhile, cook the potatoes in salted water until tender.

Boil the peas until just done – but still bright green – and then drain and place in a blender or food processor with half the butter. Process to a smooth purée.

Drain and thoroughly dry the potatoes. Mash with the remaining butter and then add the pea purée and season to taste with plenty of salt and pepper.

Heat a heavy-based frying pan to very hot. Add the white scallop muscles (or whole scallops) and sear for 1 minute. Season, then turn the muscles over and add the corals. Cook for a further 1–1½ minutes, or until just cooked.

Meanwhile, heat the haggis until piping hot (I do this in the microwave by cutting it open and scooping the contents into a microwave bowl, covering it with clingfilm and cooking for few minutes, stirring often).

To serve, place a mound of pea mash on to each warm plate and top with a spoonful of haggis and three scallops.

Venison steaks
with brambles

SERVES 4

4 venison loin steaks/medallions

2 tablespoons olive oil

1 tablespoon raspberry or red wine vinegar

1 × 200g tub crème fraîche

1 heaped tablespoon Dijon mustard

2 teaspoons red currant jelly

125g / 4½ oz brambles (blackberries)

IT IS CRUCIAL with venison – whether you are cooking a whole haunch or a little steak – never to overcook it, as it is very lean and can become tough. Cooking steaks is easy and cooking times ought to be calculated primarily on thickness, not weight. The cooking times given below are for a steak about 3cm/1¼ in thick. If your steaks are thicker, increase the time by a couple of minutes; decrease for thinner. But even the thickest steak will only take 15 minutes in total: for both the browning/cooking in the pan and the resting in the low oven. Remember always to err on the side of undercooking; you can always pop them back in the oven for another couple of minutes if they are too rare. Serve with jacket potatoes and stir-fried cabbage or broccoli.

~

Preheat the oven to 150°C / 300°F / Gas 2.

Remove the meat from the fridge a good half hour before cooking. Rub all over with 1 tablespoon of olive oil and season.

Heat a heavy-based frying pan to hot, add the remaining oil, and then place the steaks in the pan. Cook for 2 minutes on one side. Reduce the heat to medium, turn and cook for a further 1½–2 minutes. Remove to an oven plate and place in the oven, uncovered, for about 6 minutes to rest.

Meanwhile, place the pan back on the heat and stir in the vinegar. Once it is bubbling away, add the crème fraîche, mustard, jelly and berries. Simmer over a medium heat, stirring, until slightly thickened (4–5 minutes), crushing some berries into the sauce. Season to taste and then serve with the steaks, some potatoes and cabbage or broccoli.

Chocolate and whisky mousse with Bride's Bonn

SERVES 6

200g / 7 oz dark chocolate
(minimum 60% cocoa solids)

50g / 1¾ oz unsalted butter, diced

2 tablespoons malt whisky

150g / 5½ oz mini marshmallows

1 × 300ml tub double or whipping cream

DURING A FIVE-DAY holiday on Shetland, we decided to invite our friends Isabel and Martin Johnson round for dinner. Pudding had to be quick but I wanted it to have a little Scottish flavour. I achieved that by adding some whisky to a chocolate mousse recipe – and also by serving the little mousses with Bride's Bonn. I make this simply by incorporating some medium oatmeal into my shortbread recipe (see on page 106): use 150g / 5½ oz flour and 50g / 1¾ oz medium oatmeal instead of 200g / 7 oz flour.

Bride's Bonn is a traditional Shetland cake or bread – formerly it was a sweet, oat bannock and then later a thick round of shortbread. This was broken over the bride's head by the womenfolk as she entered the house for the wedding party after the church service. The idea behind it was rather like confetti these days, but guests would scrabble for pieces of the shortbread to take home and put under their pillows – they were meant to have special attributes to enhance dreams. Which is why Bride's Bonn was also traditionally known as Dreaming Bread.

If you don't have time to make Bride's Bonn, then serve the mousses with good buttery shortbread.

~

Place the chocolate, butter, 1 tablespoon of the whisky and the marshmallows in a microwaveable bowl and heat until everything is melted, taking it out to stir often. Allow to cool for a few minutes.

Meanwhile, whip the cream with the remaining whisky to soft peaks.

Fold the cream into the chocolate mixture a little at a time at first, and then fold everything together gently until smooth.

Spoon into six little glasses (it is rich) and leave for an hour or so in the fridge.

Serve with Bride's Bonn or shortbread.

Burns Supper and St Andrew's Night

Chapter 5

Cheap Midweek Supper

SOMETIMES A SPOT of frugality is called for in the kitchen but implicit in this is that taste is not compromised. Here are some ideas for inexpensive but tasty suppers; dishes that will not break the bank. Instead of buying prime cuts of meat, buy cheaper braising cuts and casserole them slowly until meltingly soft and tender. Eschew those exotic fish from foreign waters and opt for our own local herring, whiting or mussels. Give imported fruit and veg a miss for a while and choose local, seasonal fruit and vegetables instead. Bulk out meals with carbohydrates, such as bread, rice and pasta. Don't confine simple foods, such as eggs or black pudding, to the breakfast table but zap them up into a delicious supper dish. Make use of all the bits and pieces in your cupboards and larder. And if, like me, you have a secret sweetie and chocolate supply, raid this to make easy puds, by mixing Crunchies with whipped cream (see page 39) or melting down some of your hidden Toblerones and spooning over ice-cream.

Turkish eggs with spinach and dill

SERVES 2–4

225g / 8 oz spinach, washed

3 tablespoons olive oil

25g / 1 oz fresh dill, chopped

4 large free-range eggs

200g / 7 oz Greek yoghurt

1 fat garlic clove, peeled and finely chopped

½ teaspoon paprika

½ teaspoon crushed chilli

THIS IS INSPIRED by a lovely Turkish dish of poached eggs with spiced yoghurt called *Cilbir*. The spice *kirmiza biber* (a crushed chilli blend) is heated with butter then this is poured over poached eggs covered with garlicky yoghurt. My version is quick but also practical as it is easier to cook in the oven – you can start the minute you walk in the door and, 15 minutes later, once you have changed into something comfortable and perhaps poured yourself a glass of wine, it will be ready. Unlike poached eggs, it needs no supervision.

—— ∼ ——

Preheat the oven to 180°C / 350°F / Gas 4.

Wilt the spinach in a large pan with 2 tablespoons of the oil; this will take no more than 3 minutes. Remove from the heat and add the chopped dill. Season and tip into a gratin dish.

Make four indentations in the spinach and break an egg into each one. Season each egg lightly and place in the oven for 10 minutes, or until the whites are just set.

Meanwhile, beat together the yoghurt, garlic, spices and 1 tablespoon of oil with a pinch of salt. Carefully dollop this in between the eggs and then place the dish back into the oven for a further 3–4 minutes; the yolks should be cooked but still runny.

Eat at once with plenty of good bread.

Stornoway black pudding and tomato pizza

200g / 7 oz strong white flour

1 heaped teaspoon easy-blend yeast

1 tablespoon olive oil, plus extra for drizzling

semolina

5–6 tablespoons passata

5–6 thin slices Stornoway black pudding

8–10 cherry tomatoes, halved

100g / 3½ oz mozzarella, sliced

THIS IS WONDERFUL served with a salad of crunchy leaves (Cos or Romano lettuce, or chicory), dressed in a vinaigrette made with grainy mustard. And if you have never made pizza before, don't be put off; pizza dough is a doddle. But don't forget to put your oven on well in advance: set it as high as it will go!

Sift the flour into a bowl, mix with the yeast and ½ teaspoon of salt, and then make a well in the centre. Add the oil and enough warm water to form a soft dough – about 150ml / 5 fl oz. Combine to a dough with your (floured) hands and place on a floured surface. Knead for 8–10 minutes, shaking over some more flour, if necessary, until the dough is smooth and elastic. Place in a bowl, cover and leave somewhere warm (an airing cupboard is good) for 1½–2 hours, until well risen.

Preheat the oven to 250°C / 500°F / Gas 9 – or as hot as it will go.

Punch down the dough a couple of times to deflate. Sprinkle some semolina on to your work surface and then tip out the dough. Roll out with a rolling pin (lightly, do not press too hard) and stretch out gently, until you have a large, thin round, about 30cm/12 in diameter. Place this on a large round pizza stone or baking tray, which you have dusted with semolina to prevent sticking.

Smear the passata over the dough and then top with the black pudding. Scatter the cherry tomatoes all around and then top with the cheese. Season with black pepper and drizzle with olive oil.

Bake in the preheated oven until crispy and golden on the crust – about 10–12 minutes. Serve piping hot.

Stornoway black pudding

Charles Macleod Butchers, in Stornoway on the Isle of Lewis, produce some of the best black pudding in the land. About twenty-five years ago they were producing 300 black puddings a week by hand; now they produce well over 3,000, having switched to more automated production. Even so they can scarcely keep up with demand. Stornoway black pudding is both earthy and sophisticated, homely and stylish: it has a good clean flavour, crispy outside, is soft within and has no discernible globules of fat, which I find so unpleasant in French *boudins*.

There is a distinctive Hebridean taste to this versatile Scottish product, even though it has changed from the days when most crofts made their own *marag dhubh* (Gaelic for black pudding) after a sheep was killed. Nowadays fresh sheep's blood is never used.

Charles Macleod Butchers was opened in 1947 by the original 'Charley Barley'. After he died in 1967, his sons Iain and Charles took over the business and have built it up from a tiny shop to a large premises that includes an extensive delicatessen and mail-order facilities.

Scottish lamb stew

SERVES 4

1kg / 2 lb 4 oz boneless lamb chops,
trimmed of excess fat and halved
(gigot is ideal but you could also use
the cheaper neck fillet, sliced thickly)

3 onions, peeled and cut into chunks

4–5 large carrots, peeled
and cut into large chunks

1 large floury potato, peeled
and cut into chunks

2–3 sprigs thyme

600ml / 20 fl oz hot lamb stock

400g / 14 oz small waxy potatoes
(e.g. Charlotte), scrubbed

freshly chopped parsley or chives, to garnish

THIS IS MY – Scottish! – variation on a traditional Irish stew. Serve with soda scones or soda bread.

— ∼ —

Preheat the oven to 180°C / 350°F / Gas 4.

Place the meat in a frying pan and cook over a medium heat until brown. Remove with a slotted spoon and then add the onions and carrots to the pan and toss around for a minute or two in the hot fat.

In a large ovenproof dish, layer the meat, onions, carrots and floury potato – incorporating the potato near the base (these will mash into the sauce to thicken it). Season with salt and pepper, and tuck in the thyme sprigs.

Pour over the stock and then top with the waxy potatoes (these will steam and remain whole). Cover and cook in the preheated oven for about 1½–2 hours.

Remove from the oven, check the seasoning and sprinkle the parsley over the top before serving in deep bowls.

Cheap Midweek Supper

Herring fillets with cauli cheese mash

SERVES 4

16–20 cherry tomatoes

olive oil

1 small/medium cauliflower

1 large potato, peeled

8 small herring fillets (or 4 large)

90–100 ml / 3–3½ fl oz double cream

2 tablespoons good Cheddar
(I like Mull Cheddar), grated

Dijon mustard, to serve

THIS IS A truly tasty dish that is also cheap. The cauli cheese mash is worryingly moreish: you have been warned! And, though I opt for a Mull Cheddar which is more expensive than many other cheeses, it's worth buying a good Cheddar as you will need far less to add sufficient flavour. And, by the way, this is 'mash' without overdoing the potatoes!

Herring used to be called 'Silver Darlings' and in the fabulous, eponymous book by Neil M. Gunn, he describes their importance around the shores of Scotland in the early nineteenth century. After the atrocities of the Highland Clearances, the herring industry was often the only means of survival. He wrote that the silver darlings 'pushed poverty from the door and beyond the little fields'. It is sad that nowadays the herring industry is greatly depleted. But, when you see them in season, buy, cook and savour the taste of Scotland's most humble and tasty fish.

Preheat the oven to 220°C / 400°F / Gas 6.

Place the tomatoes on a small baking tray and drizzle with oil. Roast in the oven for 15–20 minutes.

Cut the cauliflower into florets and chop the potato into small pieces. Boil together in a saucepan of boiling salted water until tender (this should take 10–12 minutes), and then drain.

Heat a grill pan until hot and place the herring on it (you do not need to add any fat to the pan). Grill until done: about 2–3 minutes each side.

Tip the vegetables into a food processor and blitz with enough cream to make a smooth purée. Once blended, add the cheese and whizz again briefly to combine. Season to taste.

To serve, place a mound of mash on to individual plates and top with a herring fillet and a roasted tomato. Suggest to others they dollop mustard on the side.

Crunchie puds

SERVES 6–8

1 x 600ml tub double cream

7 Crunchies

THIS IS A very easy dessert that can be rustled up in a flash; it is best left overnight to chill and then served the next day by which time they become nice and gooey. They can also be frozen. My original recipe stipulates six Crunchies but I like to add one more for extra crunch and goo!

~

Lightly whip the cream to soft peaks.

Meanwhile bash the Crunchies so they are crushed but still have some chunks in them.

Gently fold the crushed Crunchies into the cream and then spoon this mixture into individual dishes. Chill overnight before serving.

Lemon creams

SERVES 6

1 × 600ml tub double cream

125g / 4½ oz golden caster sugar

the juice of 3 large lemons
and the zest of 1 lemon

A LEMON DESSERT is perfect at Easter to complement the rich chocolate eggs and cake! You can use half lemon, half lime here if you like, but add an extra lime as they are smaller.

~

Place the cream and sugar in a large saucepan over a low heat and bring slowly to the boil, stirring often. Once the sugar has dissolved, increase the heat to medium and bubble away gently, stirring constantly, for about 3 minutes.

Remove from the heat and add the lemon juice and zest. Stir well and then leave for 10 minutes or so, stirring now and again.

Pour into pretty little glasses and leave somewhere cool for at least 2 hours to firm up. Serve with thin shortbread fingers.

Chapter 6

Sunday Roast

SUNDAY LUNCH IS alive and well and living in the country. City-dwellers might also like the thought of the entire family sitting down to a roast haunch of venison at 1pm precisely but, really, it just doesn't happen. On Sunday mornings either everyone is abed, recovering from the night before's frivolities, or the duty parent is ferrying children from horse riding to swimming to mini-rugby. Even regular church-goers wouldn't be able to concentrate on the sermon, wondering if the teen-ager in charge of deer-basting had surfaced yet.

But Sunday evening is the ideal time for the traditional roast. There is far more time to prepare everything and you can have an extra glass of wine, knowing that all you have to negotiate afterwards are the stairs to bed and not the slopes of a hill on a brisk Sunday afternoon walk.

Whichever time of day you choose, though, do not abandon the Sunday roast! And whichever bird or meat you opt for, don't scrimp on the pudding, which should be hearty and comforting.

Spinach gratin

SERVES 4–6

300g / 10½ oz spinach, prepared

25g / 1 oz butter

25g / 1 oz plain flour

350ml / 12 fl oz milk

50g / 1¾ oz mature Cheddar, grated

40g / 1½ oz Parmesan, grated

THIS IS DELICIOUS served alongside fish, roast chicken or pork. It is also good as a vegetarian option served with bread and a tomato or chicory salad.

Preheat the oven to 350°F / 180°C / Gas 4.

Cook the spinach in a little oil or with a few drops of water until lightly wilted, and then drain.

Melt the butter in a saucepan over a medium heat and then add the flour, stirring to make a thick paste. Gradually add the milk, whisking constantly, and cook over a medium heat until smooth and thickened. Season with salt and pepper, and then stir in the Cheddar.

Combine the sauce with the spinach, grind some more black pepper over the top and tip into a shallow oven dish. Sprinkle over the Parmesan and bake for about 30 minutes, or until golden brown and bubbling.

Lamb shanks with red wine and rosemary

SERVES 4–6

4 large or 6 small lamb shanks

2 tablespoons plain flour, seasoned

3 tablespoons olive oil

1 onion, peeled and chopped

2 fat garlic cloves, peeled and chopped

2 leeks, cleaned and chopped

3 fat carrots, peeled and chopped

4 sticks celery, chopped

250ml / 9 fl oz red wine

400ml / 14 fl oz hot lamb stock

½ a 700g jar passata

2–3 thick sprigs rosemary

THIS TASTY DISH is good served with a salad and mashed potatoes or just a large sourdough loaf – for that all-essential dunking.

— ~ —

Preheat the oven to 150°C / 300°F / Gas 2.

Place the shanks in a large freezer bag with the seasoned flour and shake well to coat.

Heat 2 tablespoons of the oil in a large casserole and, once hot, add the shanks and brown all over (you may have to do this in batches). Remove from the pan and set aside.

Add 1 tablespoon oil to the pan and gently fry the vegetables, adding a little more oil if necessary.

Return the lamb to the casserole dish, pour in the wine and hot stock, and stir in the passata. Bring to the boil, add the rosemary, cover tightly and place in the oven for 2¾–3 hours.

Remove from the oven, take out the sprigs of rosemary, check the seasoning and then serve piping hot.

Lamb

On Scotland's islands it is perhaps surprising to first-time visitors how freely the sheep roam. Over the hills and glens, the roads, footpaths and beaches, they stroll around, looking so relaxed, it seems as if they are the tourists, not us.

On Lewis the native breed is the Blackface sheep ('blackies'). Although hardy, it is a small beast so it is often cross-bred with Cheviots, which are larger. The taste is superb, since the sheep graze not only on grass and heather, but also on wild herbs and flowers, all of which add to the resulting flavour.

In the Borders there are also many Blackface sheep and these are often crossed with the larger Texals. The cross-breeding of sheep is done not only for size and ease of adapting to certain land or weather conditions, but also for the temperament and character of the animal.

On the Shetland Isles the ancient Shetland breed of sheep (neolithic sheep bones reveal its ancestry here) graze on heather grassland that might contain wild flowers and herbs such as wild thyme, violets, orchids, primroses or bird's foot trefoil. Seaweed is also a part of the diet of many of the Shetland sheep, as they go to the shore to graze. Seaweed not only provides the animals with essential minerals, it also gives an additional flavour to the meat, which has been proved to have unique health-giving properties. This native Shetland breed is smaller but the meat has a truly distinctive taste.

Herb, mustard and lemon roast chicken

SERVES 4–6

1 large free-range chicken

½ onion, peeled and quartered

1 lemon

1 tablespoon Dijon mustard

5 tablespoons extra virgin olive oil

2 heaped tablespoons chopped fresh herbs

FOR THE HERBS, I recommend a couple of the following: tarragon, parsley, mint or marjoram. Serve with sauté potatoes and spinach. For roast potatoes, add chunks of peeled potatoes to the roasting tin after the first 20 minutes and turn them once.

Preheat the oven to 200°C / 400°F / Gas 6.

Place the chicken in a roasting tin. Season the insides with salt and pepper, and tuck the onion quarters inside.

Halve the lemon and squeeze the juice into a screw-top jar with the mustard, 4 tablespoons of the oil and the herbs, and shake until amalgamated. Season with salt and pepper to taste.

Tuck the lemon halves into the chicken with the onions.

Carefully slide your hand down the back bone between the chicken skin and the breast meat. Easing the skin away very gently, spread about half of the herby dressing over the breast meat, under the skin, using a teaspoon and your fingers. Pour the remaining dressing slowly over the chicken.

Roast the chicken for 20 minutes and then remove from the oven to pour the final tablespoon of oil over the top. Reduce the oven temperature to 180°C / 350°F / Gas 4 and then return the chicken to the oven for a further 20 minutes per 450g / 1 lb, basting every 20 minutes.

Check to see if it is cooked by inserting a sharp knife into the leg: the juices should run clear. Remove from the oven and allow to rest for about 15 minutes, loosely covered in foil. Carve and serve with the juices poured over.

Haunch of venison with mushroom sauce

1 boneless haunch of venison

4 tablespoons red wine

4 tablespoons olive oil

8–10 juniper berries, crushed

FOR THE SAUCE

50g / 1¾ oz dried wild mushrooms

500ml / 18 fl oz dry white wine

300g / 10½ oz fresh mushrooms
(e.g. Portobello, chestnut),
wiped and roughly chopped

50g / 1¾ oz butter

1 tablespoon olive oil

3 garlic cloves, peeled and chopped

40g / 1½ oz plain flour

1 × 150ml / 5 fl oz tub double cream

a few shakes Worcestershire sauce

WHETHER WILD OR farmed, it is a good idea to marinate a large joint of venison before cooking it. And though I normally advocate the fast-cooking method for small pieces of venison (searing in a pan then roasting at a high temperature for a brief time and then resting well), I prefer the slow-roasting method for large pieces of meat. The result will not be rare but it will be tender, succulent and well-done. It is utterly delicious with this creamy mushroom sauce and perhaps some 'skirlie potatoes' (potatoes tossed in fried oatmeal and onion) and stir-fried Savoy cabbage.

— ∿ —

Place the venison in a large, non-metallic dish. Combine the wine, oil and juniper berries, and pour over the meat. Massage the venison all over with your hands. Leave covered somewhere cool (preferably not a fridge) for a minimum of 8 hours (or overnight).

Preheat the oven to 200°C / 400°F / Gas 6.

Place the meat in a roasting tin, pour over the marinade and season with salt and pepper. Roast for 20 minutes and then turn the oven temperature down to 170°C / 325°F / Gas 3 and cover the meat with foil. Continue to cook for 30 minutes per 450g / 1 lb, basting every 15 minutes or so, if possible. When it is ready, remove the venison to a carving board (reserving the cooking juices), cover with the foil again and rest for 10 minutes or so.

Meanwhile, to make the sauce, rinse the dried mushrooms and soak in the wine for about 30 minutes.

Melt the butter and olive oil in large saucepan and gently fry the fresh mushrooms and garlic for a couple of minutes.

Drain the soaked mushrooms, reserving the wine, chop and add these to the pan. Cook over a medium heat for about 10 minutes, stirring well, then sprinkle over the flour. Cook for a further minute, stirring continuously, and then add the reserved wine. Bring slowly to the boil and then lower the heat and cook, uncovered, for about 10 minutes, stirring occasionally.

Finally, add the cream and cook for 5 more minutes or so. Stir in the Worcestershire sauce and a spoonful or two of the pan juices from the venison. Taste and season accordingly.

Serve the mushroom sauce with the venison, which I also like to moisten on the plate with a spoon of the cooking juices.

Sticky toffee pudding

175g / 6 oz dates, stoned and chopped

1 heaped teaspoon bicarbonate of soda

75g / 2¾ oz butter, softened

75g / 2¾ oz Demerara sugar

75g / 2¾ oz dark muscovado sugar

1 tablespoon black treacle

200g / 7 oz self-raising flour, sifted

2 large free-range eggs

FOR THE SAUCE

100g / 3½ oz butter

125g / 4½ oz dark muscovado sugar

1 × 300ml tub double cream

EVERYONE LOVES STICKY toffee pudding but so many people only have it when they are eating out in restaurants as they imagine it is a tricky thing to cook at home. Nothing could be further from the truth! Having tried various recipes, I have come up with this one here, which is just as good as the other, steamed version that I love – but it cooks in a mere half hour, as opposed to 2–3 hours. Though it is completely over the top, this should be served with single cream or – my favourite – good vanilla ice-cream. Yum!

Preheat the oven to 180°C / 350°F / Gas 4 and butter a wide baking dish well.

Place the dates in a bowl and cover with 300ml/10 fl oz boiling water. Stir in the bicarbonate and then leave to cool.

Place the remaining ingredients for the sponge in a food mixer, add the dates and liquid, and process until combined, scraping down the sides of the bowl.

Tip into the prepared dish (it should be no more than half-full) and bake for about 35–45 minutes or until just firm to the touch. Test by inserting a wooden cocktail stick inside; it should show some moist crumbs but no wet batter.

Meanwhile make the sauce by putting the butter, sugar and cream into a deep saucepan with a good pinch of salt and stirring regularly over a gentle heat until smooth. Bubble for a couple of minutes.

Once the pudding is done, pour about a third of the sauce over the top of the pudding and then place it under a hot grill for a couple of minutes until it bubbles.

Serve with extra sauce and single cream.

Exceedingly deep apple pie

SERVES 10

2.5kg / 5 lb 8 oz Bramley cooking apples

250g / 9 oz golden caster sugar,
plus extra for sprinkling

1 teaspoon ground cinnamon

the zest of 1 lemon

3 dessertspoons plain flour

FOR THE PASTRY

225g / 8 oz butter, diced and softened

50g / 1¾ oz golden caster sugar

2 medium free-range eggs

350g / 12 oz plain flour

THIS FABULOUS RECIPE is based on one from Jacky Scot from Brue on the Isle of Lewis, who supplies the delightful Morvern Art Gallery with her delicious pies and cakes. It takes a long time but, believe me, it is worth all the effort.

Make the pastry by creaming the butter and sugar together, and then beating in one of the eggs and the second egg's yolk (reserve the egg white for glazing). Stir in the flour. (Or make the pastry in a food processor: whizz together the flour, sugar and butter, then add the eggs while the machine is running.) Bind the dough together with your hands, wrap in cling film, chill in the fridge for about 45 minutes.

Meanwhile, core, peel and slice the apples. Lay the slices on 2–3 large trays lined with kitchen paper and leave for about 45 minutes: they will go brown but don't panic. This dries them out, intensifying the flavour.

Preheat the oven to 180°C / 350°F / Gas 4 and butter a deep 23cm / 9 in cake tin. Roll out two thirds of the pastry and line the base and sides of your cake tin. Roll out the rest of the pastry to make a lid. Keep to one side.

Put the sugar, cinnamon, lemon zest and flour in a bowl and mix together. Blot the apples dry with kitchen paper and tip them into the bowl with the cinnamon mixture. Combine thoroughly. Place the apples in the pastry-lined cake tin, squashing down with your hands. Don't worry, they will all go in! It might just look a little bulgey.

Dampen the pastry with water and then top with the lid. Press the edges together. Trim off any excess pastry.

Whisk the reserved egg white lightly and then brush over the top of the pie. Sprinkle with caster sugar and make two slits in the lid. Place in the preheated oven for about an hour, covering loosely with foil after half an hour to prevent the top burning.

Serve warm with ice cream or custard.

Chapter 7

Easter Lunch

EASTER IN SCOTLAND was never celebrated as much as in England. We had egg-rolling down hills and egg-painting for decorations, but the traditions were less important. I do, however, vividly recall the Easter Bonnets. My sister and I had little straw hats that were decorated with flowers and each year these would be dusted off and worn to church. After church there would be egg-rolling and the hard-boiled eggs would be eaten with a picnic. Chocolate Easter eggs were minimal and inconsequential, compared to the overload nowadays. (I say that as one who, soon after Christmas, is already deciding which type of chocolate egg I would like for Easter!)

These days, Good Friday is when the festivities begin, usually with a wonderful fish pie (see page 68 for a great fish pie recipe). Hot cross buns are served during the whole weekend and Easter Sunday lunch is always lamb.

I love Easter – not only for its association with chocolate – but for the simplicity of its traditional food, compared to the massive hype that is too often associated with Christmas feasts. The message of Easter is also one of the most uplifting in the Christian calendar.

Here is a menu for Easter Sunday lunch, with a lovely chocolate cake for tea.

Smoked salmon rolls

MAKES 30 'ROLLS'

3 soft tortillas or floury wraps

approx 85g / 3 oz cream cheese
(low fat is fine)

150g / 5½ oz smoked salmon

horseradish relish/sauce
and snipped dill, optional

the juice of 1 lemon

YOU CAN PREPARE these little pinwheels a day in advance and cut them simply into neat little pieces on the day. They are the perfect nibble to serve alongside Easter fizz!

~

Lay out the tortillas and spread each one with cream cheese.

Lay the smoked salmon slices on top and then squeeze over a little lemon juice. You can also dot a little horseradish on top and sprinkle on some freshly snipped dill at this stage if you wish.

Roll up the wraps, as tightly as you can, to make a sausage. Wrap tightly in clingfilm and refrigerate until needed.

Just before serving, remove the clingfilm and slice thinly into little rolls or pinwheels.

Smoked salmon

Cold-smoked salmon is more traditional than hot-smoked. Though production varies, the method is more or less the same whether it is done by hand or by machine: a whole side of salmon, pin-boned, has salt rubbed all over (some are brined), before being left for 10–12 hours. The salt is then rinsed off, the salmon is soaked in fresh water for 20 minutes, and then left on racks to dry thoroughly – overnight if possible. Finally the marinade is rubbed in (usually by hand, even if it is mass-produced salmon) and the sides are smoked over oak or beech chips for a couple of days: the drier it becomes, the easier it is to slice. Freshly smoked salmon is a true gourmet feast, whether plain or flavoured with a spiced marinade.

Roast lamb with cannellini beans, roasted garlic and cherry tomatoes

SERVES 6–8

1 large leg lamb

4 large / 8 small garlic bulbs,
plus 3 peeled cloves

5 tablespoons olive oil

6–8 stalks cherry tomatoes on the vine

1 large onion, peeled and chopped

500g / 1 lb 2 oz dried cannellini beans,
soaked overnight

500ml / 18 fl oz hot lamb stock

2 fresh bay leaves

START THE DAY before by soaking the beans. (Or you can cheat by using a couple of tins of beans – if you do this simply add them to the pan of sautéed garlic.) Serve this with a good loaf of bread for dunking and a green salad for after.

——— ∼ ———

Preheat the oven to 220°C / 425°F / Gas 7.

Make sure the lamb is at room temperature and then put it in a roasting tin. Cut 8–10 slits all over. Slice 2 of the peeled garlic cloves into slivers and insert these into the slits. Season well and then rub over 1 tablespoon of oil. Place in the preheated oven for 15 minutes.

Cut the top quarter or so off each unpeeled garlic bulb, by slicing horizontally across the top. After the meat has been in for 15 minutes, remove it from the oven and add the garlic to the tin, tucking the bulbs around the meat. Drizzle a tablespoon of oil over the garlic, reduce the heat to 190°C / 375°F / Gas 5 and continue to cook for 15 minutes per 450g / 1 lb, basting once.

Some 20–30 minutes before the end of the cooking time, place the cherry tomatoes (still on the vine) on top of the garlic bulbs and continue cooking.

Meanwhile, to make the beans, heat 3 tablespoons of oil in a saucepan and gently fry the onion. Chop the remaining garlic clove and add this to the onion.

Rinse the drained beans and add them to the pan, stirring well.

Pour in the hot stock, and add the bay leaves and plenty of ground pepper (no salt). Bring to the boil and boil rapidly for a couple of minutes. Cover, reduce to a simmer and cook for about an hour or until the beans are tender. Just before serving, check the seasoning and add some salt, if necessary.

Allow the lamb to rest for at least 10 minutes before carving and serving with the roasted garlic, tomatoes and a spoonful or two of the beans.

A great, big, fudgy chocolate cake

SERVES 8–10

300g / 10½ oz unsalted butter, softened

150g / 5½ oz golden caster sugar

150g / 5½ oz light muscovado sugar

250g / 9 oz self-raising flour, sifted

3 rounded tablespoons cocoa powder, sifted

4 large free-range eggs

½ × 400g tin condensed milk

FOR THE FILLING

75g / 2¾ oz butter, softened

200g / 7 oz golden icing sugar, sifted

1 heaped tablespoon cocoa powder, sifted

1–2 tablespoons milk

FOR THE TOPPING

100g / 3½ oz dark chocolate

½ × 400g tin condensed milk

chocolate mini eggs, to decorate

THIS DELICIOUS CAKE is moist, rich and fudgy. Perfect for Easter Sunday tea!

Preheat the oven to 190°C / 375°F / Gas 5 and butter and line a 23cm/9 in spring-form cake tin.

Put the butter, sugars, flour, cocoa powder, eggs, half the tin of condensed milk and a pinch of salt into a food mixer. Starting on slow speed, beat until smooth – this should take a couple of minutes. Increase the speed once the flour has settled down into the mix and it is not flying everywhere.

Spoon the mixture into the prepared cake tin, smoothing the surface. Bake for 15 minutes, then turn down the oven to 170°C / 325°F / Gas 3 and continue to bake for a further 30 minutes, or until a cocktail stick inserted into the centre comes out clean. Cover the top loosely with foil for the last 20 minutes or so.

Remove to a wire rack, loosen the edges and release the sides, but leave the cake on its base to cool completely. Cut in half carefully horizontally through the middle.

To make the filling, beat the butter, icing sugar and cocoa powder together, adding a tablespoon or two of milk, enough to make a creamy consistency. Spread on top of one half of the cake and then cover with the other half of the cake.

Put the chocolate and the other half of the condensed milk into a microwaveable bowl and heat for only a minute or so until the chocolate has melted, and then stir until smooth. Slowly pour over the top of the cake and spread out carefully. Decorate with mini eggs.

Chapter 8

School Traybake Sale

IF YOU ARE still lucky enough to be allowed to provide home-baking for the kids at school, then watch just how quickly it disappears. There is nothing better than home-baked cakes, traybakes, biscuits and tarts. If you are worried about the time it takes to bake, then think about this: a scone takes five minutes to prepare and ten minutes to bake; a flapjack takes five minutes to prepare and a mere twenty minutes to bake – both a good deal quicker than driving to the supermarket to buy dodgy, additive-laden baked goods. Home-baked also means pure, unadulterated ingredients and you get to be the arbiter of how much sugar and fat go in – if you want less fat in a cake, then go for it! By using unrefined sugar it is also a less unhealthy treat.

All baking can be frozen once cooled. Carefully wrap it up and pop it in the freezer. It'll be ready to be taken out whenever you have people in or a school fair to provide for. Get baking – it's not only therapeutic, it's also delicious and comforting. Heaven on a tea plate!

Chocolate bar slab

200g / 7 oz butter

6 tablespoons golden syrup

250g / 9 oz milk chocolate
(minimum 30% cocoa solids)

150g / 5½ oz dark chocolate
(minimum 60% cocoa solids)

500g / 1 lb 2 oz digestive biscuits, crushed

500g / 1 lb 2 oz Rolos and Toblerones
(5 tubes Rolos; 2 Toblerone bars
– not the giant ones!)

FOR THE TOPPING

250g / 9 oz milk chocolate
(minimum 30% cocoa solids)

50g / 1¾ oz dark chocolate
(minimum 60% cocoa solids)

THIS INDULGENT RECIPE is also fabulous for picnics as it is not at all fragile – and everyone loves it!

Line a 23 × 33cm / 9 × 13 in Swiss roll tin with baking parchment.

Melt the butter, syrup and milk and dark chocolates together; I do this in the microwave, though you can do it in a saucepan over a medium heat.

Stir in the crushed biscuits and then gently fold in the Rolos. Tip into the Swiss roll tin and spread evenly.

Bash the Toblerone triangles a little to break them up and then dot the pieces all over, pushing down into the mixture.

Melt the chocolate for the topping in the microwave and then spread all over. Leave to cool then cut into slabs.

Cranberry, coconut and seed oaty flapjacks

MAKES 18 BARS

175g / 6 oz butter

3 tablespoons golden syrup

150g / 5½ oz light muscovado sugar

350g / 12 oz porridge oats

50g / 1¾ oz plain flour

½ teaspoon bicarbonate of soda

50g / 1¾ oz dried cranberries

50g / 1¾ oz desiccated coconut

25g / 1 oz sunflower seeds

25g / 1 oz pumpkin seeds

YOU CAN ADD other seeds and dried fruit, just be sure to stick more or less to the quantities here. And you can omit the flour and use all oats, if you prefer (in which case use 375g / 13 oz oats); this gives a slightly chewier texture. It isn't as easy to cut into neat slices, but it is perfect for those who need to avoid wheat flour.

Preheat the oven to 180°C / 350°F / Gas 4 and lightly butter a 23 × 33cm / 9 × 13 in Swiss roll tin.

Melt the first three ingredients together in a saucepan over a low heat or in a microwave.

Stir in the oats, flour, bicarbonate of soda and a pinch of salt.

Add the remaining ingredients, stir well, and tip into the prepared tin, spreading out to level the surface.

Put the tin on a large baking tray (in case of spillage) and place on the middle shelf of the oven until golden brown but still slightly soft (about 18–20 minutes). Remove the tin to a wire rack and cut into bars while it's still hot, but only remove the flapjacks from the tin once they're cold.

Oats

'A grain, which in England is generally given to horses, but in Scotland supports the people,' was how Dr Samuel Johnson, the eighteenth-century essayist and lexicographer, defined oats in his famous dictionary. This was a dig at the prevailing Scottish poverty, but it also accurately described the virtual monopoly oats have had in the Scottish diet for centuries.

As a Scot, I was brought up on oats. There were oatcakes, flapjacks, bannocks and, of course, porridge. Soups were thickened with oatmeal; apple crumbles topped with oatflakes; and one of our favourites was skirlie, made from toasted oats and onion.

With the increasing awareness nowadays of the valuable contribution oats play in a healthy diet, we all ought to be making more of an effort to include oats in our everyday diets. A low-GI (Glycaemic Index) cereal, oats are high in zinc, protein, iron, B vitamins, calcium and cholesterol-reducing soluble fibre – so why not begin each day with porridge?

Coconut and chocolate slab

500g / 1 lb 2 oz chocolate (I like milk and dark mixed – aim for at least 30% cocoa solids for milk chocolate and 60% for dark)

225g / 8 oz icing sugar, sifted

225g / 8 oz butter, softened

1 × 400g tin condensed milk

just under 450g / 1 lb desiccated coconut

400g / 14 oz *dulce de leche* (or caramel made by simmering an unopened 400g tin of condensed milk in a covered, heavy-based saucepan for 2 hours, topping up the water often)

a good handful of Rice Krispies

THIS OUTRAGEOUSLY RICH traybake is based on one I enjoy at Porto & Fi, my nearby café in Newhaven, Edinburgh. They call theirs Honeymoon Slice and it sells like hot cakes!

Line a 23 × 33cm / 9 × 13 in Swiss roll tin with grease-proof paper.

Melt half the chocolate in a microwave and pour into the prepared tin, spreading evenly over the paper. Leave to set.

Cream the sugar and butter together, and then add the condensed milk and the coconut, combining well. Carefully spread over the chocolate, levelling off.

Pour the caramel over the top (you might need to warm it slightly to make for easier pouring) and finally sprinkle with the Rice Krispies.

Melt the remaining chocolate and carefully spread this on top. Leave until really well set before cutting into slabs.

Jam and coconut tart

MAKES 16–20 SLICES

400g / 14 oz sweet shortcrust pastry

approx 12 tablespoons jam (or *dulce de leche*)

10 ginger biscuits, crushed

175g / 6 oz golden caster sugar

175g / 6 oz desiccated coconut

75g / 2¾ oz semolina

3 large free-range eggs

Jam

Jam plays a part of many Scots' childhood memories. Like me, many will recall the sweet alluring aroma of jam bubbling away in a pan after a session of berry picking. As young teenagers, many Scots went, as I did, 'to the berries' (mainly in Angus and Perthshire) to gain some extra pocket money by picking strawberries, raspberries, blackcurrants and gooseberries.

We also had berries in the garden – raspberries and some blackcurrant bushes – so I vividly recall the fabulous smell of boiling jam in the kitchen with wasps flying madly around. The berries were boiled with equal quantities of sugar until setting point was reached: a teaspoon would be tested by leaving it to set on a cold plate. Then it was time to get the girdle on to make pancakes to eat warm with the freshly boiled jam.

THIS RECIPE IS based on one of my childhood favourites but was also inspired by a gorgeous cake I had in Buenos Aires. The Scottish version has strawberry jam (we always used home-made) under a coconutty layer, but the Argentinean cake had a thick layer of *dulce de leche*, that deliciously moreish caramel spread that most of South America is obsessed by! I have also added a layer of ginger biscuit crumbs for extra crunch and flavour.

Lightly butter a 23 × 33cm / 9 × 13 in Swiss roll tin.

Roll out the pastry to fit the Swiss roll tin. Prick over the base with a fork and leave to chill for a few hours (or freeze for an hour).

Preheat the oven to 190°C / 375°F / Gas 5.

Line the pastry with foil and baking beans, and bake blind for 15 minutes. Remove the foil and beans, and bake for a further 5 minutes.

Spread the jam (or *dulce de leche*) over the base and then sprinkle over the biscuit crumbs.

Mix together the remaining ingredients and then spoon this carefully over the top. Gently pat out to cover.

Bake for 20 minutes until golden brown and then remove to a wire rack to cool. Cut into slices and serve warm with clotted cream for pudding or cold with a cup of tea.

Ant cake

200g / 7 oz butter, softened

175g / 6 oz golden caster sugar

3 large free-range eggs

225ml / 8 fl oz advocaat

250g / 9 oz self-raising flour, sifted

1 × 100g tub chocolate vermicelli

KIDS LOVE THIS – not just for the name but also for the taste! And, in fact, adults do, too, as it is a delightfully moist cake with a terrific colour from the yellow advocaat. The recipe was given to me at a book signing recently by a German lady called Helga who said this was a family favourite back home in Germany. Don't worry about giving to children with advocaat in the recipe – any alcohol disappears once cooked!

— ∼ —

Preheat the oven to 180°C / 350°F / Gas 4 and butter a 24cm / 9 in round spring-form cake tin.

Beat the butter and sugar together until creamy, and then gradually add the eggs, beating well after each one.

Pour in the advocaat, and add the flour and vermicelli. Combine well but gently.

Spoon into the prepared cake tin and bake in the oven for 35–40 minutes, until firm to touch and the edges have started to come away a little. Remove to a wire rack to cool in the tin before taking away the base and sides. This needs no icing as it's very moist with the many flecks of chocolate throughout – which, of course, resemble ants!

Treacle tart bars

350g / 12 oz sweet shortcrust pastry

1 × 450g tin golden syrup

1 heaped tablespoon black treacle

the zest of 2 unwaxed lemons
and the juice of 1 lemon

100g / 3½ oz white breadcrumbs
(I like sourdough about a day old)

2 large free-range egg yolks, beaten

1 × 300ml / 10 fl oz tub double cream

TO MY MIND, these are better than a classic treacle tart, which is basically golden syrup, breadcrumbs and lemon. My version not only comes in handy bar shape but is also less teeth-stickingly sweet, as it is lightened with cream and eggs. It also has a wonderful colour from the black treacle: the real thing and one of Scotland's favourite ingredients.

Roll out the pastry to fit a lightly buttered, shallow 20 × 30cm / 8 × 12 in rectangular baking tin. Prick with a fork and then chill well.

Preheat the oven to 200°C / 400°F / Gas 6.

Bake the pastry blind by lining with foil and beans and baking for 15 minutes. Then remove the foil and beans and cook for a further 5 minutes. Take out of the oven to cool and turn the oven temperature down to 170°C / 325°F / Gas 3.

Meanwhile, gently warm the syrup and treacle (I do this in a microwave on medium; or in a saucepan over a very low heat), and then stir in the lemon zest and juice.

Tip in the breadcrumbs, combining well, and then add the beaten egg yolks and stir.

Pour in the cream and then, once everything is fully combined, tip into the pastry case and bake for about 35–40 minutes, or until there is a slight wobble in the centre. Leave to cool before cutting into 12 bars.

Carrot cake cupcakes

MAKES 12

250g / 9 oz carrots (approx 2 large carrots)

150g / 5½ oz light muscovado sugar

150ml / 5 fl oz vegetable oil

3 large free-range eggs, beaten

150g / 5½ oz self-raising flour

1 rounded teaspoon ground cinnamon

1 level teaspoon bicarbonate of soda

the zest of ½ orange

100g / 3½ oz raisins

FOR THE FROSTING

300g / 10½ oz cream cheese

the zest of ½ orange

55g / 2 oz icing sugar, sifted

YOU CAN TOP each of these delicious cupcakes with a fresh raspberry in summertime, if you like.

— ∼ —

Preheat the oven to 180°C / 350°F / Gas 4 and put twelve cupcake paper cases in a muffin tin.

Peel and finely grate the carrots. (It is important they are not coarsely grated.)

Using a balloon whisk, whisk together the sugar and oil, and then gradually whisk in the eggs.

Sift together the flour, cinnamon and bicarbonate of soda, and fold these into the mixture using a wooden spoon.

Stir in the orange zest, grated carrot and raisins, and combine thoroughly.

Spoon the mixture into the paper cases and bake in the preheated oven for about 20 minutes, or until well risen (a wooden skewer inserted into the middle of a cupcake should come out clean). Remove to a wire rack to cool.

Beat all the frosting ingredients together and then use to ice the cakes.

Chapter 9
Feeding the Team

PICTURE THE SCENE: the football or rugby team are due to arrive for food. Will it be slimline healthfood or some hearty grub to satisfy the hunger of the superfit athletes? Loads of rib-sticking fare to fill them up, perhaps? Well, not necessarily...

Gone are the days when sportsmen's food was pure stodge and the drink mainly beer. These days, serious sportsmen are advised by a nutritionist to ensure they have adequate carbohydrates in their diet for energy, whether that be pasta, bread or grains. At a professional level, each player, depending on his position, has different requirements but, overall, there is far more emphasis on healthy eating and the team is aware that a good diet means best performance. On the day before a big match, their diet features carbohydrates but also protein. On the morning of the game, breakfast would include porridge or muesli with dried fruit, and perhaps toast with scrambled eggs or lean bacon. Shortly before the game, snacks such as energy bars are fine, but most crucial is hydration and so fluid intake is measured carefully. Even after the game players cannot tuck straight into a rich feast but must follow the protocol for recovery, ensuring they are fully rehydrated.

Presuming you are not entertaining the team shortly before a big game, feel free to have hearty fare on offer but include plenty of carbs and protein, as well as healthy salads on the side. And, provided you square it with the coach first, some beer should also be fine. Although, moderation is now the buzzword among serious sportsmen – changed days!

Fish pie

SERVES 6–8

1.5kg / 3 lb 5 oz skinless fish fillets
(haddock/cod/coley/ling and
undyed smoked haddock)

600ml/20 fl oz whole milk

25g / 1 oz fresh parsley (stalks and leaves)

8–10 peppercorns

60g / 2¼ oz butter

60g / 2¼ oz plain flour

100ml / 3½ fl oz dry white wine

3 heaped tablespoons capers

the zest of 1 large lemon

3 large free-range eggs, hard-boiled and sliced

FOR THE TOPPING

1.8kg/4 lb potatoes and parsnips/celeriac,
peeled and cut into chunks

60g/2¼ oz butter

milk for thinning, if necessary

25g/1 oz freshly grated Parmesan

I HAVE GIVEN suggestions for the white fish fillets to use for this pie; but I also sometimes add in a couple of salmon fillets, for both flavour and colour. I usually use half smoked fish, half unsmoked. And, for the topping, I like to use about two-thirds potatoes to a third either parsnips or celeriac. Serve with peas or roasted fennel. (This dish can be prepared a day in advance – just cover and chill after topping with the potato. Be sure to bring it back to room temperature before cooking, though.)

Place the fish in a saucepan with the milk. Add the parsley stalks and peppercorns, and bring slowly to the boil. Bubble for 2 minutes and then remove from the heat, cover and leave for about half an hour.

Meanwhile, to make the topping, boil the potatoes (and parsnips/celeriac) until tender, and then drain thoroughly. Mash with the butter until soft (adding a little milk if it is too thick) and then add the cheese. Season to taste.

Strain the fish liquor over a bowl and break the fish into large chunks. Place these in a large ovenproof dish.

Melt the butter in a saucepan over a medium heat and then add the flour. Cook, stirring, for 1–2 minutes and then gradually add the wine and milk, whisking until smooth. Cook for about 5 minutes and then remove from the heat and add the capers and lemon zest. Chop and add the parsley leaves. Taste for seasoning.

Place the egg slices on top of the fish and then tip over the sauce.

Spoon the mash over the fish, level with a knife and then fork up. Place on a baking tray (in case of spillage) and then bake in the oven for about 1 hour or until piping hot and golden brown. Leave for 5 minutes before serving.

The perfect cheese scone

MAKES 10 LARGE SCONES

450g / 1 lb plain flour

2 rounded tablespoons baking powder

125g / 4½ oz butter, cubed

250g / 9 oz mature Cheddar, grated,
plus 2 heaped tablespoons for topping

pinch of cracked black pepper (optional)

1 teaspoon dried mustard powder

2 large free-range eggs

approx 150ml / 5 fl oz milk

2 heaped tablespoons grated Parmesan

Wherever I go throughout the land, I am on a mission: to seek out the definitive cheese scone – light and airy but with no chemical aftertaste (some use too much baking powder, as well as self-raising flour, to make them rise) and with a good cheesy flavour, without being heavy and dense. Some are flecked with seeds; some have a strong mustardy taste.

One that I found, which is well-nigh perfect, is made by Fiona MacKinnes, chef and owner, with her brother Andrew, of Porto & Fi, a fabulous café in Newhaven, ten minutes from my house. Fiona sometimes adds paprika or herbs such as thyme, or feta and olives; she also often sprinkles them with sesame or poppy seeds just before baking. Another superb version comes from my friend Beverley Tricker; she adds dry mustard powder to hers and always sprinkles the tops with extra cheese. I have found that a mixture of Cheddar and Parmesan on top gives the perfect cheesy crust. Beverley likes to eat hers warm, buttered and with a slice of tomato on top.

Here is my own version, a combination of Fiona's and Beverley's. Hopefully you will agree it is the best cheese scone recipe! They freeze well so, even though this batch seems large, bake and freeze leftovers and you'll have one ready to accompany a bowl of soup or a summer salad at any time. If you are using cracked black pepper, be generous as dark flecks running through the scone will add even more appeal.

Preheat the oven to 220°C / 425°F / Gas 7 and lightly butter a baking tray.

Sift the flour and baking powder into a large bowl and then rub in the butter.

Stir in the cheese and add a pinch of salt, the pepper (if using) and the mustard powder.

Place the eggs in a measuring jug, stir lightly and then add enough milk to make up to 300ml /½ pint. Stir again and then add this to the bowl.

Bring the dough together gently, getting stuck in with your hands (you do not need to knead), and then place on a floured surface. Pat out until the dough is about 2.5–3cm/1–1¼ in thick. Using a fluted cutter, cut out 10 large scones and place them on the baking tray.

Brush the tops with any liquid left in the jug (add a splash more milk, if necessary) and then sprinkle with the Parmesan and extra Cheddar. Bake near the top of the preheated oven for about 12 minutes or until golden and well-risen.

Remove to a wire rack and leave until barely warm before splitting and spreading with butter.

Mull Cheddar

When the Reades moved to the island of Mull from Somerset in 1983 to farm dairy cows, they could hardly have envisaged that the small cheeses they began to make in a bucket would end up being sold in huge 22kg truckles and be in such demand they can barely keep up. But Chris and Jeff Reade manage admirably to maintain high standards with their award-winning Isle of Mull cheese. And, although they knew about milk and dairy farming, they had to learn cheese-making from scratch. Their cheese is made in the dairy that dates back from the early 1800s and came with Sgriob-ruadh Farm, near Tobermory. The milk from their Friesian-cross Brown Swiss cows is unpasteurised and is made into a cheese that is matured for at least 10 months in their cellars. It is made to a traditional Cheddar-making recipe and so is defined as 'Cheddar-style' but it differs from Cheddar because, according to Chris, 'It is a product of *here*.' The water and soil are different, as are the herbs and the draff (a by-product of ground-up malted barley from Tobermory's distillery) that the cows eat. All of this gives the cheese a unique character.

Savoury pancake layer

SERVES 6

1 teaspoon oil

450g / 1 lb lean lamb or beef mince

2 tablespoons tomato purée

a few good shakes Worcestershire sauce

50g / 1¾ oz butter

50g / 1¾ oz flour

450ml / 16 fl oz milk,
plus 1 tablespoon for thinning

1 large chicory or ½ iceberg lettuce,
shredded finely

5 thin pancakes / crêpes, about 18cm / 7 in
in diameter

approx ½ a 700g jar passata

2 heaped tablespoons grated Cheddar cheese

FOR THE CRÊPES in this recipe, I make a batch with 125g / 4½ oz sifted plain flour, a pinch of salt, 1 large egg and 300ml / ½ pint milk – this makes about eight thin crêpes. (The kids can eat the extra with lemon and syrup!)

— ∼ —

Preheat the oven to 200°C / 400°F / Gas 6 and butter an ovenproof dish.

Heat the oil in a saucepan and fry the mince gently until browned.

Add the tomato purée and cook for about 15 minutes, over a low heat. Season with salt and pepper and Worcestershire sauce.

Meanwhile, make the white sauce by heating the butter. Add the flour, cook for a couple of minutes, stirring, then slowly add the milk, a little at a time, still stirring constantly, until it has all been incorporated and you have a thick sauce. Remove two tablespoons of the liquid and keep to one side.

Stir the chicory/iceberg into the remaining sauce and season well.

Place one crêpe at the bottom of the prepared dish and spread it with 1 tablespoon of passata. Spoon over half of the chicory/iceberg sauce and then place another crêpe on top. Spread this with some more passata and then top with half of the mince. Repeat these layers with the remaining white sauce and mince.

Thin down the reserved tablespoons of white sauce with approx 1 tablespoon of milk. Place the final crêpe on top of the dish, spoon over the thinned white sauce, sprinkle with the cheese and bake in the middle of the oven for about 20 minutes, until golden brown on top.

Serve at once, cut into wedges, with salad.

Meat pie

SERVES 4–6

2–3 tablespoons olive oil

900g / 2 lb stewing/casserole beef, diced

2 heaped tablespoons plain flour,
seasoned with some salt and pepper

1 onion, peeled and finely chopped

2–3 carrots, peeled and diced

500ml / 18 fl oz hot beef stock

1 heaped tablespoon tomato purée

1 tablespoon Worcestershire sauce

FOR THE PASTRY AND GLAZE

150g / 5½ oz strong white flour

150g / 5½ oz plain flour

175g / 6 oz butter, diced
(or 100g / 3½ oz butter and 75g / 2¾ oz lard)

1 medium free-range egg, beaten

YOU CAN MAKE the pie double crusted or just have a pastry lid. And you could also use good, butter puff pastry instead of home-made shortcrust. The stew for this pie is best made the day before – if you don't quite manage that, just make sure it has cooled to room temperature before putting into the pie.

First make the stew by heating 1 tablespoon of the oil in a wide saucepan. Toss the beef in the seasoned flour and then brown in the pan. Remove with a slotted spoon and then add the rest of the oil. Gently fry the onion and carrots for a few minutes and then return the meat to the pan with the hot stock, tomato purée and Worcestershire sauce. Stir and lower the heat to its lowest setting, cover and cook on the hob (or in a preheated low oven – 150°C / 300°F / Gas 2) for 1½ hours, stirring once. Remove from the heat, taste and adjust the seasoning, and then cover and chill overnight once cold.

To make the shortcrust pastry, sift the strong and plain flours into a food processor and add the butter. Whizz briefly until it resembles breadcrumbs, and then add a couple of tablespoons of cold water – just enough to bring the mixture together with your hands. Wrap in clingfilm and chill for half an hour.

Preheat the oven to 200°C / 400°F / Gas 6 and place a baking tray inside to heat up.

Roll out two thirds of the pastry to fit the base and sides of your pie dish. Fill with the cold stew. Roll out the remaining pastry to make a lid and seal the edges.

Brush with the beaten egg and snip a small hole in the top with scissors. Chill for half an hour or so while the egg sets.

Place the pie directly on to the heated baking tray (so the shortcrust pastry base begins to cook immediately) and bake in the oven for 15 minutes. Reduce the heat to 180°C / 350°F / Gas 4 and continue to cook for a further 40–45 minutes, covering loosely with foil for the last 15 minutes or so.

Serve piping hot with lots of broccoli or spinach.

Chapter 10

Saturday Night TV Suppers

SATURDAY NIGHT IS the ideal night for TV viewing (or getting out a good DVD) and enjoying some delicious food on your lap and perhaps the odd can of beer or glass of wine. And, though this is the time many of us resort to takeaways, I reckon it is just as easy to rustle up something tasty and delicious yourself in a flash. It is also a great deal cheaper.

Some dishes need no cutlery at all, some only a fork or spoon; whatever you choose to cook make sure it is sofa- or armchair-friendly. Then serve up generous portions, sit back and align your knees to balance your tray or plate on your lap, press the remote and enjoy a fabulous Saturday night in!

Haggis nachos

½ haggis

1 × large bag of tortilla chips (or pitta chips)

1 × large tub salsa

handful of jalapenos, sliced

good handful of grated Cheddar

1 × large tub sour cream

1 × large tub guacamole

handful of fresh coriander, roughly chopped

THIS RECIPE IS based on one that Jo Macsween demonstrated when she and I did a double act at a cookery demonstration in Glasgow. What a brilliant concept haggis nachos are – and so quick and easy. I have added grated cheese to Jo's delicious recipe. This is very messy: napkins are essential! Serve with cold beer or margaritas.

——— ~ ———

Heat the haggis in the microwave by cutting it open and disgorging the contents into a microwave bowl, covering it with clingfilm and cooking for few minutes, stirring often, until piping hot.

Meanwhile, empty the bag of tortilla chips on to a large plate. Dollop generous spoonfuls of salsa over the chips and add a few jalapeños.

Once the haggis is piping hot, dot spoonfuls on top of the nachos, then top with the cheese. Place under a hot grill until melted and bubbling

Spoon over some sour cream and guacamole, and sprinkle with roughly chopped coriander to finish. Eat immediately with a beer or margaritas.

Partan bree risotto

SERVES 3–4

approx 850ml / 1½ pints hot fish
(or light chicken) stock

50g / 1¾ oz butter

1 medium onion, peeled and finely chopped

1 large stick celery, finely chopped

7–8 anchovy fillets, chopped

300g / 10½ oz risotto rice
(I prefer Carnaroli, though Arborio is also fine)

1 × large glass dry white wine

350g / 12 oz crab meat (mainly white), cooked

2 tablespoons freshly chopped parsley

freshly grated Parmesan (optional)

Partan bree

This is a rich, creamy crab soup thickened with rice: *partan* means crab, *bree* means liquid or gravy. If you can, a large live crab should be used as your base: boil it for 15–20 minutes and then remove the creamy brown (body) meat to one bowl and the sweet white (claw and leg) meat to another. Discard the feathery 'dead men's fingers' as you work. Otherwise, fresh or defrosted frozen crabmeat will do.

Typical in many seaside areas of Scotland, Partan Bree of course has regional variations. Lady Clark of Tillypronie in her cookbook from 1909 suggests adding some anchovy (presumably anchovy essence); I also rather like a shake or two of Worcestershire sauce. It is also traditional to add a blade of mace for extra flavour.

THIS TASTY DISH has the elements of a Partan Bree soup and is truly delicious as a comforting bowl on your lap on a Saturday night. A crisp chicory salad served after would make it more healthy!

——— ∾ ———

Bring the stock to a simmer in a large saucepan.

Meanwhile, heat two thirds of the butter in a large risotto pan or deep frying pan, add the onion and celery and cook gently over a medium heat for 8–10 minutes until softened.

Stir in the anchovies and cook for another minute or so.

Add the rice and stir until coated in the fat and beginning to make a slight crackly sound as it 'toasts'.

Pour in the wine, increase the heat and leave to bubble for a couple of minutes. Reduce the heat to medium again and gradually add the hot stock, ladle by ladle, stirring well and only adding more liquid once the previous ladleful has been absorbed.

After about 15 minutes, add the crab meat and season with some pepper (no salt needed as the anchovies are salty). It should be ready after 18–20 minutes – the rice will be *al dente* (firm yet tender). Taste and check the seasoning.

Add the remaining butter, stir well and then cover and leave to stand for 5 minutes.

Finally, stir in the parsley, check the seasoning again and serve straight from the pan, with or without Parmesan.

Chicky mêlée

SERVES 2–3

3 tablespoons olive oil

1 leek, cleaned and finely sliced

4 slices black pudding, skinned

1 tablespoon pine nuts

1 tablespoon raisins

1 × 400g tin chickpeas, drained

1 tablespoon freshly chopped parsley

1 tablespoon balsamic vinegar

THIS GUTSY DISH is based on a wonderful dish I had in Barcelona, which was basically chickpeas with *morcilla* – black pudding.

So here is my interpretation, which I named after a game my dad used to play in the Dundee of his youth called Chicky Melly. In Angus the game got its name from The Auld Alliance because, though 'Chicky' is English (as in – you are chicken or cowardly if you don't do something), 'Melly' is from the French *mêlée*, referring to the ensuing fracas if you were caught! It was basically a game of ringing doorbells then running away but my dad and his brother and sisters used to play another more intricate – and exceedingly naughty – version. In my dad's own words this is what the tenement lads and lassies of Dundee used to play in the 1920s and 30s:

'You need a large, loaded screw, a swing-top bottle's rubber washer and a long length of stout string. Wrap the string round the threads of the screw then place the screw inside the rubber washer. Lick the washer (yes, lick – saliva helps adhesion better than water!) and stick this on the window of the person you want to annoy (the ultimate effect was of an irritating rattling on the window). Immediate retreat of Chicky Melly boys and girls with the other end of string to Baxter Park opposite. Through the railings, pull the string taut and strum, as on a double bass (to activate the incessant window tapping), then run away when the person looks out the window or when the park warden arrives...'

— ∿ —

Heat the oil in a frying pan and gently sauté the leeks until soft. Push to the sides of the pan and increase the heat a little.

Add the black pudding to the centre of the pan and brown the slices on each side, reduce the heat to low and then add the pine nuts, raisins, chickpeas and parsley, stirring to heat through. (It doesn't matter if the pudding breaks up.) Taste for seasoning and then remove from the heat and stir in the vinegar.

Serve warm with bread.

Stornoway surf and peat

SERVES 2–3

4 tablespoons olive oil

2 onions, peeled and chopped

115g / 4 oz chorizo, cut into chunks or slices

500g / 1 lb 2 oz tiny new potatoes, scrubbed

1 glass white wine

large handful of cherry tomatoes

2–3 fillets hake, cod or monkfish, skinned

1 lemon

freshly chopped parsley, to garnish

OK, CORNY NAME but it's the Lewis version of surf and turf: fish with meat. Peat cutting has been making a revival on the Outer Hebrides because of the increased price of oil and the idea for this dish came from a wonderful meal I enjoyed at the Crowberry Guest House, a haven of luxury and good taste in the village of Bac, north of Stornoway. Owners Lisa and Alasdair Maclean primarily cook using local ingredients. Alasdair's family have owned the house for years and so his contacts with local fishermen means he can find out what is best on the day. He cooked this dish for us with locally landed hake but he also uses monkfish or cod, again both local. I like it with herring fillets, too: simply grill them for a couple of minutes on each side, and then serve on top of the potatoes.

—— ～ ——

Preheat the oven to 170°C / 325°F / Gas 3.

Heat 2 tablespoons of oil in a large frying pan and sauté the onions for 10 minutes or so over a gentle heat.

Add the chorizo and stir until coated. Season with salt and pepper to taste.

Stir in the potatoes, pour over the wine and then cover and simmer for 15 minutes, or until the potatoes are almost tender.

Transfer to an ovenproof dish and add the tomatoes. Place on the high shelf of the preheated oven, uncovered, for about 30–40 minutes, or until the potatoes are slightly caramelised and the tomatoes are about to burst.

Meanwhile, place the fish in another ovenproof dish and squeeze over some lemon juice and 2 tablespoons of oil. Season with salt and pepper and place on the low shelf of the preheated oven, once the potatoes have been in for 10 minutes. Bake for 20 minutes until just cooked but tender.

To serve, spoon some of the potatoes on to individual warm plates and then top with the fish.

Chapter 11

Book Club Supper

BOOK CLUBS ARE the Tupperware parties *de nos jours*! Both men and women like them – my husband's book club meets in the pub. There – I am told – they order their pints and get down immediately to the business of discussing the book in question. This discussion goes on all night. The ladies' book club I am member of, however, meets at someone's house where we take a good couple of hours to catch up on news and gossip over a glass or two of wine before the food comes out and someone finally suggests we discuss the book. Ah yes, the book... This discussion can take anything from 10–30 minutes and then the next book is chosen by democratic means.

Though the *raisin d'être* of our monthly meetings is ostensibly to discuss a book, I like to see the ladies meeting as more of a general philosophical chat about the human condition. I have a feeling the boys down the pub might have other words to describe our soirées, though!

Here are some ideas for easy dishes you can cook when you have the girls round.

Strawberry and red wine risotto

SERVES 4–6

approx 600ml / 20 fl oz hot
light chicken (or vegetable) stock

2 tablespoons extra virgin olive oil

½ red onion, peeled and chopped

200g / 7 oz strawberries, hulled and quartered

150g / 5 oz risotto rice
(I prefer carnaroli, though Arborio is also fine)

½ × large glass red wine

50g / 1¾ oz grated Parmesan

THIS LITTLE-KNOWN TUSCAN dish is usually made with wild strawberries but since freshly picked Scottish strawberries – preferably from a Pick Your Own farm – are so divine, they are perfect for this risotto. And it looks pretty fabulous, too! Serve with a well-dressed salad.

— ∼ —

Bring the stock to a simmer in a large saucepan.

Meanwhile, place the oil in a large frying pan and gently sauté the onions over a medium heat until soft.

Add half the strawberries, stir and then add the rice, stirring to coat in the fat.

Pour in the wine and cook until evaporated. Reduce the heat to medium/low and start adding the hot stock a ladle at a time, only adding more liquid once the previous ladleful has been absorbed. Stir often, adding some salt after 10 minutes or so. You will need just enough stock so that the rice is *al dente* and the risotto creamy.

Once it is ready, remove from the heat and stir in the cheese and remaining strawberries. Cover and leave for a couple of minutes.

Just before serving in warm bowls, add plenty of freshly ground black pepper and salt, if necessary.

Strawberries

As a child, I was one of that happy band of berry-pickers who were paid a paltry sum of money to pick berries all day long in sun, rain or wind, during the summer. In Angus and Perthshire school holidays and berries were inextricably linked. Hordes of schoolchildren would walk, cycle or catch a bus to 'go to the berries'. It was a way of life and the irritating scratches and red-stained t-shirts were part and parcel of it.

On arrival at the fruit farm in the morning, we would collect our buckets (called luggies) and tie them round our waists with string. Then we would be dispatched to the fields – mainly for raspberries but, depending on the length of the season, it could be strawberries, which were the best of the lot as they were so tasty. The rows of berries, called dreels, would be full of youngsters putting the ripe red berries into their luggies. The only downside was that the picking gave you a sore back. So, at the end of a long, weary berry-picking day we would queue up at the weighing area. I was never surprised to find that I had earned very little money, since most of my berries seemed to have gone into my mouth rather than my luggie!

Red pepper and goats' cheese tart

2 red peppers

1 tablespoon olive oil

1 onion, peeled and chopped

1 × 150g log of goats' cheese, sliced into rounds

200ml / 7 fl oz crème fraîche

3 large free-range eggs

FOR THE PASTRY

200g / 7 oz plain flour

50g / 1¾ oz grated Parmesan

150g / 5½ oz butter, diced

1 medium free-range egg

THIS VERY EASY tart relies on the subtle flavour of goats' cheese combined with the bold flavour of red peppers. I always grill the peppers first, not only to give them a nicely charred taste but also to help when it comes to removing the skin, which I find rather indigestible.

To make the pastry, whizz the flour, Parmesan and butter together in a food processor and then add the egg and whizz again until clumps are formed. Bring together with your hands and cover with clingfilm. Chill in the fridge for a couple of hours.

Butter a 23cm/9 in loose-bottomed flan tin.

Roll out the pastry and line the prepared flan tin. Prick the base all over and then chill again, preferably overnight.

Preheat the oven to 200°C/400°F/Gas 6.

Bake the pastry case blind, using foil and baking beans, for 15 minutes. Remove the foil and beans, and cook for a further 5 minutes. Take it out of the oven and reduce the temperature to 180°C/350°F/Gas 4.

Meanwhile, prepare the peppers: cut into quarters, discarding the stalk and all the seeds. Place on a grill tray and grill until charred and black. Wrap in foil for 10 minutes or so, and then remove the skins and cut the peppers into slivers.

Heat the oil in a frying pan over a medium heat and sauté the onion until soft and golden.

Once the pastry case is out of the oven, scatter the onion over the base and then arrange the peppers, spoke-like, on top.

Place the rounds of goats' cheese over these.

Whisk together the crème fraîche and eggs, and season well. Pour this over the goats' cheese and bake for 25–30 minutes, or until the filling is set. Eat warm with a salad.

Pineapplenut Pudding

SERVES 6–8

100g / 3½ oz butter, softened

150g / 5½ oz icing sugar, sifted

2 large free-range eggs

1 teaspoon vanilla extract

2 × 400g tins pineapple chunks, drained

300g / 10½ oz ginger biscuits, crushed

2 large bananas, sliced

55g / 2 oz flaked almonds, toasted

1 × 300ml / 10 fl oz tub double cream, lightly whipped

1 × 200ml tub crème fraîche

A WONDERFUL 1980's revival, this. Known in my ancient recipe book as *Gryfe Gateau* (why?), it was a confection of margarine, cream, crushed pineapple and ginger biscuits. I have substituted butter for margarine and have had to whizz pineapple chunks into a purée, since tins of crushed pineapple seemed to have died along with *Dynasty* shoulder pads. But the overall taste and luxuriously creamy texture is the same. All women love this pudding, so it's ideal for any girls' get together. Remember to make the day before serving.

— ∼ —

Cream the butter and sugar together and then beat in the eggs and vanilla until creamy. Either do this vigorously by hand or in a food processor.

Whizz the drained pineapple to a purée using a blender.

Lay a third of the ginger biscuit crumbs in the bottom of a large glass trifle bowl. Top with the creamed butter mixture and then add a further third of biscuit crumbs. Spoon the pineapple over this and then scatter on the bananas and nuts.

Combine the cream and crème fraîche gently and then spread this over the top.

Finally sprinkle with the remaining ginger biscuit crumbs, cover and chill overnight.

Chapter 12

Quick Midweek Meals

FAST FOOD NEED not be dull food. Just because you have only half an hour to produce a meal, doesn't mean you have to resort to supermarket ready-meals or dubious packets of indeterminate ingredients that require nothing more than a kettle of boiling water. It simply involves some forward planning – and quality produce. Whereas coarser vegetables, less lean cuts of meat or more elderly game can be transformed into glorious feasts by long, slow pampering on the stove, fast food depends on top-quality ingredients, which will immediately bond with your chosen complementary flavours to make truly good eating.

Salads are such a good adjunct to quick suppers at any time of the year and, as you prepare the salad dressing, bear in mind this Spanish proverb: 'The salad-maker must be a spendthrift for the oil, a miser for the vinegar, a statesman for the salt and a madman for the mixing.'

I've not suggested any pudding here; however if, like me, you have a sweet tooth, grab some fruit or a tub of your favourite ice-cream afterwards.

Salmon with soy

SERVES 2

1 tablespoon soy sauce

1 tablespoon Worcestershire sauce

1 tablespoon olive oil

2 salmon fillets, skinned

ALL THIS NEEDS is some freshly cooked broccoli and some basmati rice or – even quicker – a good loaf of bread.

Preheat the oven to 220°C / 425°F / Gas 7 and place a baking sheet on a shelf towards the top to heat up.

Mix the soy, Worcestershire sauce and olive oil in a shallow dish and then add the salmon, turning to coat. Leave for 15 minutes or so, until the oven has reached full temperature (and while you start to prepare the broccoli and cook the rice, if using).

Remove the salmon from its marinade, draining off (but retaining) most of the marinade, and place on the hot baking sheet. Do not season (there is enough salt in soy sauce) and place in the preheated oven.

Remove after 5 minutes (put your broccoli on to cook now) and slowly pour over the reserved marinade. Return the salmon to the oven for a further 3–5 minutes, until it is just cooked. Test by inserting a sharp knife into the thickest part: it should be just cooked and flake into large chunks easily.

Serve on warm plates with the sauce poured over the top, and rice and broccoli on the side.

Quick fish with roasted tomato tabbouleh and crisp Parma ham

250g/9 oz cherry tomatoes
(preferably plum)

250g/9 oz bulgar wheat

4 thick fish fillets, skinned

3 tablespoons extra virgin olive oil,
plus extra for drizzling

the juice of 2 large lemons

75g / 2¾ oz fresh parsley / coriander / mint
(or a combination of two of these), chopped

4 slices Parma ham

FOR THE FISH, I would use saithe (coley), cod or haddock, or the middle fillets of salmon. If the white fish fillets are not a middle cut, then tuck the tail/thin end underneath to make a thicker 'parcel'. You can leave out the Parma ham, if you prefer, but it gives a great flavour boost and a nice crunchy texture.

— ~ —

Preheat the oven to 220°C / 425°F / Gas 7.

Place the tomatoes on a small baking tray, drizzle with oil, season with salt and pepper, and pop near the top of the preheated oven for 15–20 minutes.

Meanwhile, boil the kettle and place the bulgar wheat in a wide shallow bowl. Pour over 500ml boiling water, cover and leave for 15 minutes.

Place the fish on another baking tray and drizzle with some oil. Season with salt and pepper and then place near the top of the oven (moving the tomatoes to a lower rack, if necessary) for 8–10 minutes until cooked through.

Meanwhile, drain the wheat of any excess water and then stir in the lemon juice, 3 tablespoons of oil, 1 teaspoon of salt, the chopped herbs, the cooked tomatoes and their juices.

Heat a non-stick frying pan to hot, then add the Parma ham (without any added fat) and fry for a couple of minutes until crispy, turning once.

Scoop little piles of tabbouleh on to individual warm plates and top with the fish. Top each piece of fish with the crispy ham and serve at once.

Crab linguini

2 tablespoons olive oil

1 fat garlic clove, peeled and chopped

1 teaspoon dried chilli flakes

large handful of cherry tomatoes, halved if large

1 × 400g tin tomatoes

250g / 9 oz linguini

125g / 4½ oz fresh white crabmeat

2 tablespoons freshly chopped parsley

the zest of 1 small orange

ON A TRIP to the Outer Hebrides, we ate some very fine crab. We visited Kallin Shellfish and bought some fresh crabmeat, which we ate on the beach in a tattie scone sandwich! (Two tattie scones clamped around the crabmeat and a tub of fresh mayonnaise coleslaw – delicious!) We also bought some boiled crab claws at their little shop at Grimsay, North Uist. It was late afternoon and the weather stunning, so we thought we would stop and have them as pre-prandials with a drink. Unfortunately all we had was some warm white wine, as the temperature had been unnaturally hot. So I asked the girl at the shop for some ice and she gave me some gauze-wrapped ice cubes. We presumed it was normal ice so we cut off the gauze and plopped the cubes into our wine, only to discover strange bits floating upwards: they were cubes of iced gel which rendered the wine sadly undrinkable. The crab was, however, delicious and a glass of water made a sobering substitute for the wine!

Heat the oil in a pan over a medium heat and sauté the garlic and chilli for a minute or so. Add the cherry tomatoes, stir and then tip in the tinned tomatoes. Season with salt and pepper, and leave to cook while the pasta boils.

Cook the linguine in a large pan of boiling salted water according to the packet instructions.

Just before you drain the pasta, add the crabmeat to the sauce, and stir well to heat through. Check the seasoning, add the parsley and orange zest and toss with the drained linguine. Serve in warm bowls.

Hairy tattie fishcakes

SERVES 4

approx 350g / 12 oz undyed smoked haddock fillets

1 large potato, peeled and cut into chunks

40g / 1½ oz butter

1 heaped tablespoon Dijon mustard

1 small free-range egg, beaten

1 heaped tablespoon flour

4 heaped tablespoons medium oatmeal
or fine breadcrumbs

sunflower oil for frying

Hairy Tatties

During visits to the Northern and Western Isles, you see packs of salted fish – salt haddock, whiting, tusk and ling – in both butcher's and fishmonger's shops. Salt cod and ling were traditionally the most common but cod is scarce nowadays. Tusk is a member of the cod family and has been very popular in Orkney and Shetland. The salt fish is soaked, boiled and then eaten with mashed potatoes and melted butter (or roasted mutton fat on Shetland).

In Aberdeenshire salt fish is used for a traditional dish called Hairy Tatties, which is mashed potatoes with flakes of boiled salt fish mixed throughout. The name derives from the technique of constantly beating the tatties to make them dry and almost fibrous (or hairy) in texture. Houses in the coastal villages would have a barrel in the back shed filled with salt herring (saaty herrin), which were served with tatties and a mustard sauce.

THIS IS A quick dish if you have the fish ready cooked, and even quicker if you use leftover mashed potato. But even if not, it can still all be done within about half an hour. Using oatmeal instead of making breadcrumbs also hastens the procedure. I have taken the liberty of using smoked haddock instead of salt fish, which is what is traditionally used in hairy tatties, since salt fish needs soaking and so takes longer.

First cook the haddock by lightly poaching in a little milk or grilling with a pat of butter, until just cooked (4–5 minutes), then flake into chunks.

Meanwhile, boil the potato chunks until tender and drain thoroughly. Mash with the butter, mustard and plenty of salt and pepper to taste.

Add the flaked fish and combine gently with the potatoes. Check seasoning. Form into four fishcakes and chill well, preferably for a couple of hours, or pop in the freezer for 5 minutes.

Set out three plates in a row. Put the egg in one and the flour in another and the oatmeal or crumbs on the final plate. Dip each cake in egg, then flour and then oatmeal. The fishcakes can be put back in the fridge again at this stage if you don't want to eat them immediately – they can be made a day or so in advance.

Heat some oil in a shallow frying pan over a medium heat and, once it is hot, fry the fishcakes for 2 minutes on each side until golden. Lower the heat to medium and continue to fry until cooked through – a further 10 minutes or so.

Serve with salad.

Scallops with duck eggs

SERVES 2

6 scallops

3 tablespoons extra virgin olive oil

225g / 8 oz prepared spinach

2 duck eggs

ONE SUNNY, WARM day on the Outer Hebrides, I popped into the shop at Kallin Shellfish in the tiny harbour at Grimsay on North Uist. Their crab-meat, lobster and scallops are fabulous, all sourced from the waters of the Western Isles and around the shores of Skye. Chatting to local man Hector Stewart, who runs Kallin Shellfish, was interesting. Even though many of us have only come to appreciate scallops relatively recently, as they are so often seen on restaurant menus now, people living on the shores have eaten them forever. When he was growing up on North Uist, they would sometimes be able to 'fish out' scallops with a scoop at low tide on a fine, clear day; since they are usually in deep water, it was difficult to see them otherwise. His mother would pour a kettle of boiling water over them to open the shells and then she would fry them in butter and serve them with a fried egg – duck or hen – the yolk of which acted as the sauce.

This dish is not only quick, it is also delicious. Serve it with boiled new potatoes, if you have time. And, if not, a good loaf of sourdough bread.

Toss the scallops in 1 tablespoon of olive oil and leave for half an hour or so before seasoning.

Cook the spinach until just wilted; I do this in the microwave, which takes 3–4 minutes.

Heat a griddle pan to searing hot.

Meanwhile, put a frying pan over a high heat, add 2 tablespoons of oil and then, once smoking hot, crack in your eggs. Leave for 2–3 minutes and then remove from the heat and season: the residual heat will continue to cook them. (They should have runny yolks and cooked whites that are crispy at the edges.)

Pop the scallops on to the hot griddle and cook them for a minute or so on either side, until just cooked through.

To serve, place some spinach in the middle of each individual warmed plate, top with a duck egg and then place the scallops around. Eat them dipped into the yolks. Yum!

Black pudding with goats' cheese and grilled peppers

2–3 red or yellow peppers

4 slices black pudding (I like Stornoway, Macsween or Ramsays of Carluke)

4 slices goats' cheese (approx same circumference as the pudding)

3 tablespoons extra virgin olive oil

1 tablespoon balsamic vinegar

EAT THIS WONDERFUL but simple dish with plenty of good bread and a salad.

~

Preheat the oven to 200°C / 400°F / Gas 6.

Quarter and de-seed the peppers, then place them under the grill until charred. Remove the skin and cut into slivers.

Put the black pudding on a baking tray and place on the top shelf of the preheated oven for 10 minutes. Remove and place a round of goats' cheese on top of each one and then return them to the oven. Bake for a further 5 minutes or so, to warm the cheese through, and then place under a hot grill until browned.

Toss the peppers in the oil and vinegar.

To serve, place the black pudding and goats' cheese on to individual plates and top with some peppers.

Harissa chicken with couscous salad

SERVES 2

2 chicken breasts, skin on

2 heaped teaspoons harissa paste

3 tablespoons extra virgin olive oil,
plus extra for drizzling

250g / 9 oz couscous

2 peppers (preferably 1 red and 1 yellow)

1 red onion, peeled and quartered

the juice of 2 lemons

2 garlic cloves, peeled and crushed (optional)

2 tablespoons freshly chopped mint

FIRST THING TO do is put the oven on and prepare the chicken. Only then turn to the couscous and peppers. It should all come together nicely a mere 30 minutes after entering the kitchen!

~

Preheat the oven to 220°C / 425°F / Gas7.

Slash the chicken through the skin and then rub with the harissa paste, ensuring it gets right into the flesh. Place the breasts on a baking tray, drizzle with olive oil and bake at the top of the oven for 10–15 minutes, or until cooked through.

Meanwhile, place the couscous in a wide, shallow bowl and cover with 300ml / 10 fl oz boiling water. Fork through and then cover tightly with a doubled tea-towel or clingfilm. Leave to stand for 5–10 minutes.

Quarter the peppers and remove the seeds and membrane. Place them on a sheet of foil on a grill tray with the onion, drizzle with a little oil and grill for about 10 minutes or until they are charred. Remove from the grill and cover in more foil. Leave for about 5 minutes to loosen the skin. Remove the skin from the peppers and cut into dice with the onion.

Fork through the couscous to remove any lumps and season with ½ teaspoon of salt.

Whisk together 3 tablespoons of oil, the juice of 2 lemons, the garlic and some freshly ground black pepper and pour over the couscous. Stir well and allow to cool.

Add the peppers, onion and mint to the couscous and stir. Check the seasoning and serve with the chicken.

Chapter 13

A Summer Party

A FAMILY PARTY in summertime lends itself to all sorts of possibilities. There is the barbecue option, the buffet option or a simple lunch or dinner that can be prepared as much as possible in advance. I would do away with formal starters with any party of more than twelve people and just hand round delicious canapés. Then some sort of casserole is always good, as this can be served with bread or tiny new potatoes. Don't opt for a heavy wintry dish but rather look to the hotter climes for inspiration: a Moroccan-style tagine is ideal. And, as for dessert, something seasonal, such as a currant parfait, can be made well in advance and served with good buttery shortbread... unless of course you receive offers of, 'Can I bring a pudding?' Never refuse – anything to make life easier on the day!

Crab hummus

1 × 400g tin chickpeas, drained

the juice of 2 large lemons
and the zest of 1 lemon

3 tablespoons tahini paste

1 garlic clove, peeled and chopped

1 heaped teaspoon ground cumin

½ teaspoon chilli flakes

4–5 tablespoons extra virgin olive oil

approx 150g / 5½ oz white crabmeat

some cayenne pepper and
pitted black olives, to garnish

THIS IS LIKE a regular hummus in texture and basic flavour but I have added lemon zest, chilli and some crabmeat to make it even more special.

~

Place the chickpeas, lemon juice and zest, tahini paste, garlic, cumin and chilli flakes into a food processor and whizz with a little salt and 4–5 tablespoons of oil. Once combined, add a couple of tablespoons of cold water and whizz again to get a purée consistency.

Add the crab meat and whizz – but only very briefly – until just incorporated. (You don't want to break up the crabmeat.) Taste and adjust seasoning.

Tip into a bowl and sprinkle over some cayenne pepper and surround by olives.

Serve with warm pitta or chicory leaves.

Spinach, feta and mint filo rolls

MAKES 40–50

400g / 14 oz spinach

200g / 7 oz feta, crumbled

25g / 1 oz fresh mint or dill, leaves snipped

1 large free-range egg

approx 200g / 7 oz filo pastry sheets

100g / 3½ oz butter, melted

FOR MY MOTHER-IN-LAW Hilary's eightieth birthday party, we had a middle eastern/Greek/Turkish theme as she and John, my father-in-law, spent many years in Turkey and loved the food. My lovely Greek neighbour Marco kindly made huge trays of *spanakopitas* for it using his mother Maria Dafereras' recipe. I have changed the recipe a little here, since hers was for cute individual pies, whereas mine are little rolls. Maria is a traditional Greek cook who makes everything from scratch – from bread to her own filo pastry. She also cooks octopus regularly, though nowadays she says she is too old for tenderising the cephalopod in the traditional way – by bashing it on the rocks – so does it mechanically instead by placing the octopus in the tumble drier before cooking. It works a treat!

Preheat the oven to 200°C / 400°F / Gas 6 and lightly butter a baking tray.

Cook the spinach until just wilted (in a microwave or in a pan with a few drops of water) and then drain thoroughly over a colander, squeezing dry with clean tea towels.

Chop the spinach and mix in a bowl with the crumbled feta, mint or dill and egg. Season with salt (though not too much, as feta is salty) and pepper.

Lay out one sheet of filo, brush with the melted butter and cover with a second sheet. Brush this with butter and cover with a third sheet. Finish with another brush of butter. Cut the sheets in half and lay some of the filling along the length of one half. Roll the pastry over the filling to enclose it, so you have a long sausage shape. Cut this into 5 or 6 small pieces, like sausage rolls, and place them on the prepared baking tray. Brush the tops with butter and continue with the rest of the pastry and filling.

Bake in the preheated oven for about 15 minutes or until golden and flaky.

Serve warm.

Lamb tagine with artichokes and quails eggs

SERVES 8

2 tablespoons olive oil

1kg / 2 lb 4 oz boneless shoulder of lamb (or stewing/braising beef), cubed

2 large onions, peeled and diced

2 fat garlic cloves, peeled and chopped

1 teaspoon ground cumin

½ teaspoon ground cinnamon

1 teaspoon ground ginger

1 good pinch saffron strands

400ml / 14 fl oz hot lamb (or beef) stock

1 large or 3 small preserved lemons, peeled and finely chopped

8–12 artichoke wedges from a jar of artichokes in oil, well drained

25g / 1 oz fresh coriander, chopped

8 quails eggs, fried in olive oil until soft

THIS IS BASED on a dish I had in Marrakesh. It was a tagine of lamb with dates and was served topped with a row of cute little fried quails eggs. It was sublime! I am not a great fan of dates and so have used artichokes, which are often found in tagines, instead. If you can't be bothered with the quails eggs, small hens eggs will do but it won't look quite as gorgeous.

Serve this dish with warm couscous dressed in a little olive oil and lemon juice and some freshly chopped mint.

Simply double this recipe if it is to feed more. As part of a buffet, this quantity ought to be fine for eight.

Preheat the oven to 150°C / 300°F / Gas 2.

Heat the oil in a heavy-based casserole dish over a medium heat and brown the lamb all over. Remove to a plate with a slotted spoon, and then fry the onion and garlic for about 5 minutes.

Increase the heat to high and add all the spices, stirring continually. Cook for 30–40 seconds and then add the hot stock and bring back to the boil, seasoning with some salt and pepper. Stir and, once it has come to the boil, cover tightly and place in the preheated oven for about 1–1½ hours, until the meat is tender.

Remove from the oven and stir in the preserved lemon and artichokes, and put back in the oven to continue to cook for a further 30 minutes. Taste for seasoning and stir in the coriander.

Top with the fried eggs and serve with minty couscous.

Gooseberry fool

450 g / 1 lb gooseberries, topped and tailed

50g / 1 and ¾ oz golden granulated sugar (plus extra if necessary)

the juice of ½ lemon
(or a splash of elderflower cordial)

300 ml / 10 fl oz double cream

shortbread fingers, to serve

GOOSEBERRIES ARE IDEAL to use at summer parties as they are usually available throughout the country from the end of June to August. And since they freeze well, I advise you load your freezer with them to use throughout the autumn and winter. If you are freezing it's best to top and tail them before you do, but if time is short then simply sling them in the freezer but top and tail before the berries are defrosted, otherwise they will be too squishy. To top and tail, simply snip off the top and bottom with a knife, scissors or – the most practical – your fingernails.

Could there be anything nicer than a gooseberry crumble or gooseberry pie; sweet yet sour juices dribbling through the buttery crust or crumbly topping? Well, yes, there is: a rich creamy tangy gooseberry fool – everyone's favourite.

This can also be made into ice-cream by freezing in individual ramekins for a couple of hours.

Place the gooseberries, sugar and lemon juice (or elderflower) in a saucepan and bring slowly to the boil. Taste and add more sugar if necessary. Cover, and cook gently for 5–10 minutes until just tender, then purée and allow to cool. (At this stage you can pass the mixture through a fine sieve if you want to get rid of the seeds; I prefer to keep them for a contrasting crunch.)

Lightly whip the cream then gently fold in the purée. Spoon into glasses or bowls and serve immediately or chill before serving, with shortbread.

Redcurrant parfait

2.5kg / 5 lb 8 oz redcurrants (on their stalks)

6 large free-range egg yolks

300g / 10½ oz icing sugar

900ml / 30 fl oz double cream, lightly whipped

THESE QUANTITIES CAN be divided in half for smaller gatherings.

Line two long loaf tins with clingfilm.

First put the currants (still on their stalks, though discarding any stray leaves) in a large pan with 150ml/5 fl oz water and bring slowly to the boil over a medium heat. Simmer gently for 4–5 minutes, stirring, until the currants are soft.

Drain in a colander over a large bowl, retaining the liquid. Purée the currants in a food processor (stalks and all – you are about to sieve them out) and then place this purée into a large sieve over another large bowl. Pour 400ml / 14 fl oz of the retained liquid over the berries in the sieve and push as much of the purée through as possible. You will now have about 550ml / scant 1 pint of thick but unsweetened purée. Set this aside until required.

Whisk the yolks and sugar until pale and frothy in a food mixer, then add the redcurrant purée and combine well.

Very gently but thoroughly fold in the cream until blended.

Turn the mixture into the prepared loaf tins and freeze until required.

Remove from the freezer about 20 minutes before serving. Dip the outside of the loaf tins in hot water to loosen and then cut into slices and serve with berries and shortbread.

Shortbread

MAKES 16 PETTICOAT TAILS

175g / 6 oz slightly salted butter, softened

85g / 3 oz golden caster sugar,
plus extra to sprinkle

200g / 7 oz plain flour, sifted

50g / 1¾ oz cornflour, sifted

A TRICK TO make perfect shortbread that I gleaned from my friend Aggie Mackenzie's mum Joan is not to roll out the dough to fill the tin completely but allow it to be just a little shy of the edges. That way the dough moves out during baking to fill the tin and cooks evenly.

~

Preheat the oven to 150°C / 300°F / Gas 2 and lightly butter two 18cm / 7 in sandwich tins.

Cream the butter and sugar together until really pale and creamy: this will take 4–5 minutes in a food mixer (double by hand).

Add the sifted flour and cornflour a tablespoonful at a time, only adding more when the last tablespoonful has been incorporated. When it has all been mixed in, bring the dough together with your hands and divide into two balls. Roll out each ball (either by pressing with your palms if you have cold hands or by using a very light touch with a rolling pin) to a circle just a little shy of your two prepared tins. Prick all over with a fork (ensure you go right through to the base) and 'scallop' the edges by nicking with the edge of a spoon.

Place in the preheated oven for 35–40 minutes, until a pale golden brown.

Remove the tins to a wire rack, cut each into eight triangles and sprinkle over some sugar. Leave for 15–20 minutes or so and then remove from the tins while still a little warm but firm enough to be taken out. Leave on a wire rack until cold.

Shortbread

In her book on the Scots household in the eighteenth century, Marion Lochhead writes about tea parties of the day where the hostess 'must have a plate of bun and one of shortbread – either in a cake, broken into bits, or in little, round nickety Tantallon cakes, or in the favourite "petticoat tails"...'

Over the centuries it has been made in finger-shaped biscuits, round biscuits and a full round 'cake' known as petticoat tails. The origin of the name of these dainty shortbread biscuits is interesting. Some believe it to be a corruption of the French *petites galettes*, which is taken to mean little cakes. Given the Auld Alliance and the culinary interchange between France and Scotland, this is a possibility. Or perhaps it was even more simple. Perhaps it is, in fact, to do with the shape of the biscuits: the wedges are identical in shape to the individual gores of the full, bell-hooped petticoats worn by the ladies at Court – probably at the time of Mary Queen of Scots in the sixteenth century, who was said to be fond of them.

Many years on, shortbread still appears at all the best tea parties and also at special occasions such as Hogmanay (with black bun). But it is also as regular a feature in Scottish kitchens as porridge or mince.

As for the ingredients: only the best will do. Never substitute margarine for the butter since the whole point of shortbread is its buttery taste. A dough of all plain flour makes good shortbread but you can vary this by incorporating some rice flour (for a good crunchy texture), cornflour for a melt-in-the-mouth feel, or farola (fine semolina) for a texture between the two.

Remember that shortbread should never be kneaded for longer than it takes to bring the dough together quickly in your hands. Overworking it will toughen it. Indeed, I never roll with a rolling pin, I just press out lightly to the required shape with my palms before baking. The lightest hand possible will give the lightest shortbread.

Chapter 14

Anniversary Dinner

CONTRIVED ROMANCE DOES not always work. No matter how low the lights, how moody the music, how slinky the black dress, it cannot be forced. It can, however, be helped along... Vintage champagne might cost you rather more than one week's pocket money, but it will not only help set the scene, it will also prevent hangovers the next day. Delicious yet simple food will also make the evening enjoyable and memorable.

The food should never be too rich: a little of everything, with plenty of bread to hand, in case one diner requires more sustenance than the other. Since there is no one else at the table, you can both indulge in all sorts of messy, finger-licking foods. Dipping food into interesting sauces is a good idea, too: remember the fun you used to have over the fondue set a couple of decades ago? And fun is what this is all about. Pretentious food has no place at a romantic dinner, unless you are secretly trying to give your companion the push! By all means make it look appetising, but don't over-do the plate-decorating with swirls, froths and sculpted veg.

And avoid dark green food at all costs! It matters not a jot that your teeth are a dentist's dream – perfectly straight and a dazzling, pearly white – the sight of a masticated piece of spinach lurking between your incisors is a complete and utter turn-off. So, if it has to be salad, opt for tomato.

Dessert should be simple and delicious – something that says 'Seduction on a Plate'. But if you simply can't be bothered to rustle up pudding, then just serve some fruit, such as strawberries or grapes, and melt a slab of Toblerone or some good chocolate in a bowl and get dunking. It will be thoroughly messy but, by this stage of the dinner, frankly, you won't give a damn.

Here are a couple of main course ideas, one for carnivores and one for fish-eaters.

Smoked salmon and asparagus risotto

SERVES 2 (WITH PROBABLE LEFTOVERS!)

approx 1 litre / 1¾ pints hot vegetable
or light chicken stock

approx 250g / 9 oz asparagus, washed

50g / 1¾ oz butter

1 small onion, peeled and chopped

300g / 10½ oz risotto rice (I prefer Carnaroli;
though Arborio is also fine)

100ml / 3½ fl oz dry white wine

150g / 5½ oz peas (frozen – blanch for
1 minute then drain well; fresh – cook until
just done but still bright green)

the zest 1 large unwaxed lemon

2 tablespoons grated Parmesan

150g / 5½ oz smoked salmon, cut into slivers

3 tablespoons freshly chopped mint leaves

USE LOCAL ASPARAGUS in season; otherwise just use peas. And don't forget to sling the woody ends of the asparagus (crushed slightly) into your stock as it simmers away, to increase the flavour.

——— ~ ———

Bring the stock to boil in a large saucepan.

Meanwhile, remove the woody ends from the asparagus and bash with a knife. Cut the tips off and chop the spears in two; add these (tips and spears) to the stock and boil until just tender – no more than 2 minutes depending on the thickness. Remove with a slotted spoon and set aside. Now add the woody ends to the stock and reduce the heat to a simmer. (These remain in the stock as you use it.)

Heat 25g/1 oz butter in a large pan over a medium heat and sauté the onion until soft.

Add the rice and stir until coated in the fat and beginning to make a slight crackly sound as the rice lightly 'toasts'.

Pour in the wine and cook until evaporated.

Start to add the hot stock, ladle by ladle, stirring all the time and only adding another ladle once the previous ladleful has been absorbed. After 15 minutes, add the asparagus and peas.

You may not need all the stock; it should take 18–20 minutes for the rice to be *al dente*.

Remove the pan from the heat, stir in the lemon zest, Parmesan and the remaining butter. Cover and leave to stand for a couple of minutes.

Stir in the smoked salmon and mint and check the seasoning. Cover for a further couple of minutes or so and then serve in warm, shallow bowls.

Asparagus

Throughout the spring, there is much Scottish asparagus to be devoured. According to Heather Pattullo who, with her husband Sandy, has been producing asparagus commercially in Tayside for some twelve years, the season in Scotland usually runs from early May until the third week in June. Since Pattullo asparagus is all picked at the top of the hard white part of the stem (unlike some other growers), it requires no peeling. Simply bend it until it snaps to remove the woody end – or leave it on while you cook it and use the thick end to hold between fingers and thumb as you dip the asparagus into your sauce.

Although the most popular asparagus is Select (middle thickness), the Pattullos grade theirs from Sprue (very thin) to Choice, Select, and then the fattest – Jumbo. Grading is always about size, never quality. Good local asparagus is always top quality.

Rib-eye steaks and roasted mushrooms

SERVES 2

2 well-matured rib-eye steaks

250g / 9 oz large chestnut mushrooms

olive oil, for drizzling and frying

2 tablespoons freshly chopped coriander (optional)

RIB-EYE IS PROBABLY the tastiest steak; nicely marbled and with a good 'eye' of creamy fat in the middle. The fat is where the flavour comes from. Approximate cooking times are as follows for 2.5cm/ 1 in thick steak (and this applies to any kind, whether rib-eye, sirloin or fillet): for rare – 2½ minutes each side (it should feel soft and spongy to the touch); medium-rare – 3–3½ minutes each side (it should feel soft and slightly springy); medium-well done – 4½–5 minutes each side (it should feel firm with a slight spring). A well-done steak is, to me, a waste since it will inevitably be tough. Remember to rest the steaks before eating, though, however you want them cooked.

Cooking more than two steaks at a time can be tricky, as you must never overcrowd the pan, so unless you have help – and many pans! – dinner à deux is the ideal time to splurge out on fabulous steaks. Serve with a loaf of good bread or baked potatoes and a salad of chicory dressed in a mustardy vinaigrette – and some of the salsa verde on page 190.

—— ~ ——

Bring the steaks to room temperature by removing from the fridge half an hour before cooking.

Preheat the oven to 200°C / 400°F / Gas 6.

Wipe the mushrooms clean and then place in a small baking tray. Drizzle over some oil and season. Roast in the preheated oven for about 20 minutes, or until tender, then remove and toss in the coriander, if using.

Heat a frying pan to very hot (you should feel the heat rising above it when you hover your hand there) then add a swirl of oil. Season the steaks with sea salt and coarsely ground black pepper and then fry until done to your liking (see above), turning once.

Remove the steaks to a warm plate and allow them to rest for a couple of minutes before serving with the roasted mushrooms and, perhaps, a dollop of salsa verde (see page 190).

Anniversary Dinner

Banana and lime ice-cream with chocolate sauce

SERVES 2

3 large bananas

2 tablespoons thick fromage frais

the juice and zest of 1 lime

1 tablespoon lemon juice

1 × 300ml / 10 fl oz tub double cream

150g / 5½ oz dark chocolate
(minimum 60% cocoa solids), chopped

1 tablespoon rum or brandy

THIS IS POSSIBLY the easiest ice-cream recipe ever: frozen bananas whizzed in a blender with cream and lime. That's it – no whipping or beating. Magic.

～

Place the unpeeled whole bananas in the freezer for at least 6 hours.

Remove the bananas from the freezer and leave for about 15 minutes before carefully peeling with a sharp knife. (Hold the banana firmly with a cloth.) Chop the flesh into small pieces and place in a blender with the fromage frais, lime juice and zest, lemon juice and half the cream. Process until thick and creamy, stopping the motor a couple of times to stir.

Serve immediately or place in the freezer for 30–45 minutes to firm up.

To make the sauce, melt the chocolate with the remaining cream and the rum. Do this in a saucepan over a very gentle heat or in the microwave. Whisk until smooth and serve at once with the ice-cream.

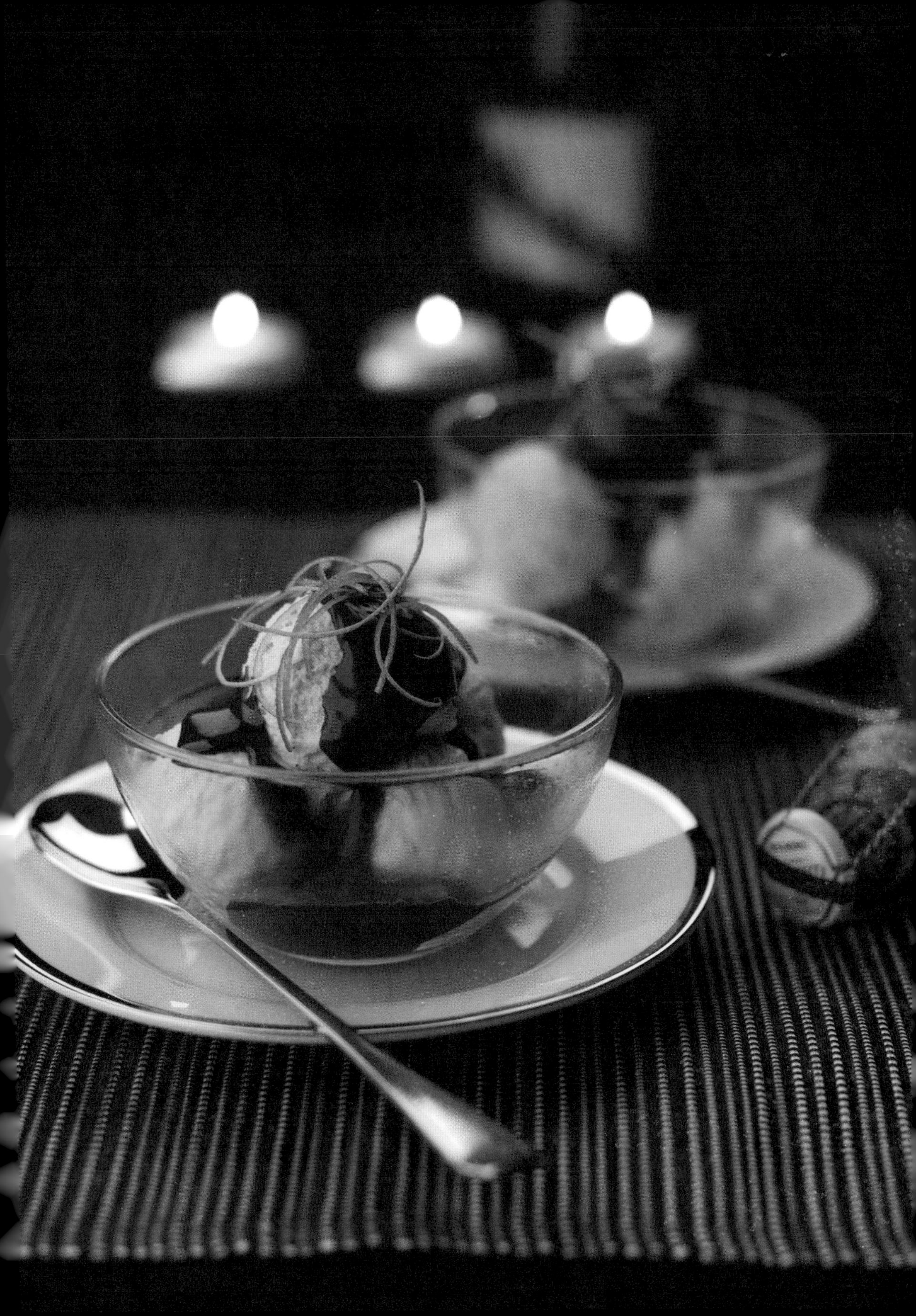

Chapter 15
Family Picnic

FAMILY PICNICS ARE the stuff of memories – photos of smiling kids with plastic cups in one hand, great big sandwiches in the other, often sitting beside a flapping windbreak on the beach or deep in the countryside with sheep looking on inquisitively.

In Scotland there are some amazing picnic venues. You might be on top of a Munro, albeit crouching down beside the trig point to get out of the wind. You could be in the remote and stunning setting of a West Coast loch. Or you might be sitting on a white isolated Hebridean beach with only some black cows strolling along the shore for company.

The main thing to remember is to take plenty of rugs and waterproofs in case the weather turns. And a thermos of hot coffee or tea is always advisable. Also – don't forget the corkscrew! You never know when the sun might come out and a chilled white wine will be called for.

Pan bagnat

SERVES 4–6

1 round loaf of good bread

1 garlic clove, peeled and halved

extra virgin olive oil, for drizzling

2 large tomatoes, sliced

1 × 200g can tuna, drained

2 large free-range eggs, hard-boiled and sliced

12–14 anchovy fillets

12–16 black olives, pitted

THIS WONDERFUL PROVENÇAL dish is perfect to take on a picnic as it can be made in advance and is delightfully messy to eat! Basically it is a salad niçoise sandwich.

Cut the loaf horizontally through the middle, removing any inner doughy bits of bread (cook's perks – or save for breadcrumbs!).

Rub the cut surfaces of the loaf with the garlic and then drizzle some olive oil over the top.

Arrange the tomatoes all over the bottom half of the loaf and place the tuna, egg, anchovy and olives on top.

Drizzle on a little more oil and then clamp on the top half of the loaf and press down gently with your hands. Leave for an hour or so and then cut into wedges and serve.

Cullen Skink pie

25g / 1 oz butter

1 small onion, peeled and chopped

1 medium potato, peeled and diced

400g / 14 oz undyed smoked haddock fillet

300ml / 10 fl oz full-fat milk

3 medium free-range eggs

2 tablespoons freshly chopped parsley
(or chives)

FOR THE PASTRY

175g / 6 oz plain flour, sifted

50g / 1¾ oz fine oatmeal

125g / 4½ oz butter, diced

1 medium free-range egg

a few drops of olive oil

SCOTLAND'S CLASSIC FISH soup, Cullen Skink, is converted into a tasty quiche here, which is ideal to take cold on a picnic or served warm at home with salad.

To make the pastry, place the flour, oatmeal and butter in a food processor, and process briefly. Add the egg and oil and process again. Bring the dough together, cover with clingfilm, and chill, preferably overnight.

Roll out the pastry to fit a buttered, deep 23cm / 9 in (or shallow 28cm / 11 in) loose-based flan tin. Prick with a fork and chill for an hour or so. Preheat the oven to 190°C / 375°F / Gas 5. Fill the pastry case with scrunched-up foil (or you could use baking beans on a layer of foil if you have them) and bake for 15 minutes. Remove the foil and cook for a further 5 minutes.

Meanwhile, melt the butter in a frying pan, then sauté the onion and potato until tender.

Poach the fish in the milk for 3–4 minutes. Strain over a jug, reserving the liquid and breaking the fish into bite-size chunks. Lightly whisk the poaching liquid with the eggs, parsley and seasoning.

Place the chunks of fish in the pastry case and then pour in the liquid. Bake for 30–40 minutes, until golden. Serve at room temperature.

Cullen Skink

The classic Cullen Skink is a fish soup made with Finnan haddock, also called Finnan haddie. The name of this cure of haddock – Finnan – is a corruption of the name of a fishing village called Findon. The haddock is left whole but with the head removed and the bone left in. It is then split (with the bone left down one side), brined and cold-smoked. It is wonderful simply grilled with a knob of butter for either breakfast or tea.

The Aberdeenshire soup can be made with whole Finnan haddock or with smoked haddock fillets – but make sure they are undyed, as the colour adds absolutely nothing. Since the soup originates in coastal Aberdeenshire (Cullen is on the north coast and Findon on the east coast, a few miles south of Aberdeen, and both are small fishing villages), I like to serve it with Aberdeen rowies (butteries).

Cottage cheese and herb muffins

MAKES 12

250g / 9 oz plain flour

2½ teaspoons baking powder

½ teaspoon bicarbonate of soda

1 large free-range egg

200ml / 7 fl oz milk

125g / 4½ oz butter, melted and then cooled

1 heaped tablespoon freshly chopped chives
(or basil or dill)

3 heaped tablespoons cottage cheese

3 tablespoons freshly grated Parmesan

THESE SOUND REALLY rather dull but you have to believe me, they are fabulous: light and moist and with a terrific flavour. Use any herbs but my favourite is chives, which seems to work well with the combination of cheeses.

The recipe is based on one from New Zealander chef Celia Harvey, who likes to vary the flavours by using, instead of cottage cheese and herbs, sun-dried tomato and Parmesan, grated apple and Cheddar, or grated cooked potato and chopped cooked sausage.

Preheat the oven to 190°C / 375°F / Gas 5 and put twelve muffin cases in a bun tray.

Sift the first three ingredients into a bowl and add a grinding of fresh black pepper and ½ teaspoon of salt.

In another bowl, whisk the egg, milk and butter, and then add the herbs.

Fold in the cheeses and add this mixture to the dry ingredients, stirring gently until blended. Do not overmix or the muffins will be tough.

Spoon into the muffin cases and bake for 20 minutes until well risen and golden.

Gooseberry crumble traybake

MAKES 12–16

600g / 1 lb 5 oz gooseberries
(red and green), topped and tailed

50g / 1¾ oz light muscovado sugar

FOR THE BASE

50g / 1¾ oz ground almonds

200g / 7 oz self-raising flour, sifted

100g / 3½ oz light muscovado sugar

150g / 5½ oz butter, diced

1 large free-range egg

FOR THE CRUMBLE TOPPING

3 tablespoons jumbo oats

3 tablespoons plain flour

3 tablespoons light muscovado sugar

2 tablespoons sunflower oil

THIS IS A great summer traybake and is ideal for the beach or an outdoor picnic as it can be a little messy. Try to use both green and red berries for added wow factor!

Preheat the oven to 180°C / 350°F / Gas 4 and butter a 23cm/9 in square cake tin.

Place the gooseberries in a saucepan with the sugar. Cook slowly over a very low heat, stirring often, until the sugar is dissolved. Cover and cook for a further 8–10 minutes, or until just tender. Remove from the heat, drain in a sieve over a bowl and allow to cool.

To make the base, place the first four ingredients in a food processor. Process until the butter is incorporated. Add the egg and process until blended. Spoon this mixture into the prepared cake tin and spread it out with a spatula, until smooth. Top with the cooled gooseberries, taking care to leave a border around the edge.

To make the topping, mix all the dry ingredients together and then stir in the oil. Scatter this all over the gooseberries, trying to make it as even as possible by pressing down gently.

Bake for about 40 minutes, or until well-risen and golden brown around the edges. Remove to a wire rack and cut into squares. Leave to cool in the tin before decanting.

Plum and orange oaty squares

MAKES 16–20

400g / 14 oz plums, stoned
and roughly chopped

the zest of 1 orange

250g / 9 oz light muscovado sugar

4 tablespoons golden syrup

300g / 10½ oz butter

350g / 12 oz porridge oats

100g / 3½ oz plain flour

THE IDEA FOR these came from a delicious traybake I tried at my local farm shop, West Craigie. It was warm out of the oven and utterly delicious!

Preheat the oven to 180°C / 350°F / Gas 4 and butter a 23 × 13cm / 9 × 13 in Swiss roll tin.

Mix the plums in a bowl with the orange zest and half the sugar.

Place the remaining sugar in a microwaveable bowl (or a saucepan over a low heat) with the syrup and butter, and heat until the butter is melted.

Add the oats and flour and a good pinch of salt, and then tip into the plums, stirring well.

Tip the mixture into the prepared tin and level out. Bake for 30–35 minutes until golden brown.

Remove to a wire rack and loosen the edges with a knife. Cut into squares while hot but leave to cool completely in the tin before decanting.

Chapter 16

Posh Picnic

OUR USUAL FAMILY picnics are seriously casual and relaxed to the point
of falling over. But just sometimes, it is nice to add some less informal
touches: proper napkins instead of a roll of kitchen paper; proper cutlery instead of fingers; and proper glasses instead of a thermos flask
and plastic cups. Take some wine and if you don't have a nearby river
or loch to chill it in, then bring a wine cooler. Set out the table, not just
on the sand or lochside but on an actual table with a tablecloth. It will
still be a fabulous outdoor feast but it will be more elegant and refined
when the occasion permits.

Like any other picnic in this country, though, don't forget to pack the
umbrellas!

Cherry tomato and olive tart

SERVES 4–6

500g / 1 lb 2 oz vine-ripened cherry tomatoes

2–3 tablespoons green or
black olive paste (tapenade)

1 fat garlic clove, peeled and finely chopped

extra virgin olive oil, for drizzling

FOR THE PASTRY

150g / 5½ oz plain flour, sifted

25g / 1 oz freshly grated Parmesan

100g / 3½ oz butter, diced

1 large free-range egg, beaten

WHEN WE WENT to see my Bermudian friend Fiona, who is married to Frenchman Giles Delassus, at her beautiful house near Carpentras in Provence, we sat outside on the terrace under the vines drinking rosé and eating a delicious tomato and tapenade tart. Though the food, scenery and hot sunshine were pure Provence, the talk was of Scotland, for Fiona was at school in St Andrews for eight years, so we talked of snow, rain and porridge!

⸻ ∾ ⸻

To make the pastry, place the flour, Parmesan and a pinch of salt in a food processor with the butter. Process briefly until the mixture resembles bread-crumbs and then add the egg through the feeder tube. Process until the mixture comes together in large clumps. Wrap the dough in clingfilm and chill for half an hour or so.

Roll out to fit a shallow 28cm / 11 in tart tin. Prick the base all over and then chill well, preferably overnight.

Preheat the oven to 200°C / 400°F / Gas 6.

Fill the pastry case with foil and baking beans, and bake blind for 15 minutes. Remove the foil and beans, and continue to cook for a further 5 minutes.

Meanwhile, cut the tomatoes in half (lengthwise if they are pear-shaped, baby plum tomatoes) and place kitchen paper on top to soak up excess moisture.

Smear the cooled pastry base with the tapenade and arrange the tomatoes on top in tight concentric circles, cut-side up. Season well with sea salt, freshly ground black pepper and the garlic.

Drizzle with oil and bake for about 30 minutes.

Remove from the oven and serve at room tempera-ture. (For the picnic, transport the tart in its baking tin.)

Fennel, mint and goats' cheese salad

SERVES 6–10

2 large or 3 medium fennel bulbs, trimmed

the juice of 2 large lemons

25g / 1 oz fresh mint, leaves removed
and chopped

40g / 1½ oz flaked almonds, toasted

150g / 5½ oz soft mild goats' cheese

3–4 tablespoons extra virgin olive oil

THIS IS A wonderfully refreshing salad that has plenty of lemon juice, not only to prevent the fennel discolouring but also to add a pleasant tang that contrasts nicely with the goats' cheese. It can be prepared in advance, but only add the oil just before serving.

— ∼ —

Shave or very thinly slice the fennel (I do this in my food processor) and place it in a bowl. Toss with the lemon juice, add the mint leaves, season with some salt and pepper, and toss again gently.

Transfer into a small serving bowl and scatter with the almonds. Roughly tear or crumble the goats' cheese over the top. (At this stage you can cover the salad with clingfilm and leave until serving.)

Drizzle the oil over the top and give it a final toss before serving. (Add a little more oil, to taste, if required.)

Celeriac remoulade with smoked venison and truffle oil

SERVES 4

1 medium celeriac

the juice of 1 large lemon

3 heaped tablespoons mayonnaise

100ml / 3½ fl oz crème fraîche

2 teaspoons Dijon mustard

100g / 3½ oz smoked venison

truffle oil, for drizzling

TAKE EVERYTHING WITH you to assemble this dish *in situ.* If you don't want the palaver of plates, drizzle the truffle oil on to the remoulade and then use the smoked venison as a wrap to hold it all together.

~

For the remoulade, peel and coarsely grate the celeriac and toss immediately in the lemon juice (otherwise it will discolour).

Mix the mayonnaise, crème fraîche and mustard together, and then stir this into the celeriac. Season, combine thoroughly and then chill.

To serve, place a little mound of remoulade on individual plates, drape over some smoked venison and drizzle with a little truffle oil.

Brioche summer pudding

1 brioche

900g / 2 lb berries (½ strawberries and the rest raspberries, blueberries, brambles and currants)

125g / 4½ oz golden caster sugar

thick cream or clotted cream, to serve

THOUGH TRADITIONALLY MADE with sliced white bread, I prefer to make summer pudding with brioche, which never goes soggy or slimy as the white bread version can!

~

Cut the brioche into thin slices and use to line the sides and base of a 1 litre / 1¾ pint pudding basin, ensuring there are no holes. (Make sure there is some brioche left over.)

Place the fruit in a saucepan with the sugar and heat gently until the sugar is dissolved. Cook for a minute until the juices run.

Using a slotted spoon, fill the brioche-lined basin with the berries and most of the juice, reserving a couple of tablespoons. Cover with the last slices of brioche, again fitting closely, and then spoon over the reserved juice.

Cover with clingfilm and place in a larger dish (in case the juices overflow) and put a weight on top (I use two tins). Once cool, refrigerate and leave overnight.

When you are ready to serve – and this is best done *in situ* for ease of transport – place a serving plate on top and deftly invert the pudding on to the plate. Cut into wedges and serve with thick cream or clotted cream.

Easiest fruit cake ever

SERVES 8–10

700g / 1 lb 9 oz mixed dried fruit
(I like just raisins and sultanas)

the juice and zest of 1 lemon

150g / 5½ oz self-raising flour

1 teaspoon mixed spice

1 large free-range egg

1 × 400g can condensed milk

THIS IS SUCH an easy recipe, similar to the boiled fruit cakes of old, but with condensed milk to make it even more moist. Because there is no butter in the cake, it is best served with a good smear of butter on top or – my favourite – with a wedge of mature Cheddar on the side.

—— ∿ ——

Preheat the oven to 150°C / 300°F / Gas 2 and line a 23cm / 9 in loose-based cake tin with baking parchment.

Place the fruit in a large pan with 125ml / 4 fl oz cold water and add the lemon juice and zest. Bring slowly to the boil over a low heat, stirring all the time. Leave to bubble for a minute or so and then take off the heat. Cover and leave to cool until barely tepid.

Once it has cooled, add the flour, spice, egg and milk and stir well. Tip into the prepared tin and smooth the surface.

Bake for about 1½ hours, covering loosely with foil after 1 hour to prevent the fruit burning. It is ready when a wooden skewer inserted into the middle comes out clean.

Remove to a wire rack and cover loosely with foil again. Leave to cool completely in the tin before turning out.

Chapter 17

BBQ in the Garden

TO SOME, A barbecue is the very embodiment of the good life – alluring aromas wafting over the garden wall and sun-drenched diners putting the world to rights over succulent char-grilled lobster and perfectly chilled Chablis. To others, it is a clutch of umbrellas hovering over desiccated – or raw! – sausages and burgers, while chattering teeth drown out every vestige of deep or meaningful conversation.

Barbecuing is, of course, the most ancient form of cooking. But it only arrived and became part of Scotland's food and social culture relatively recently. It was only with the invention of the barbecue with a lid that we have felt able to embrace a food style that requires good weather and no rain. And as we have moved away from just having burgers and sausages, we have at last established the barbecue as a part of the Scottish summer, come rain, hail or shine!

Romesco sauce

SERVES 6–8

2 large (beef) tomatoes

1 red pepper, deseeded and cut into slivers

2 whole garlic cloves, peeled

1 red chilli, de-seeded and halved

100g / 3½ oz blanched almonds

2–3 tablespoons extra virgin olive oil

1 tablespoon sherry vinegar

2 tablespoons chopped fresh coriander

6–8 thin pork chops
(or slices of halloumi cheese)

SERVE THIS FABULOUS – and easy – Romesco sauce with pork chops or halloumi. But it is also good served just as a dip, with pitta chips or tortilla chips.

— ∼ —

Preheat the oven to 190°C / 375°F / Gas 5.

Cut each tomato into four thick slices and place them on a baking tray with the pepper, garlic, chilli and nuts. Drizzle over the oil and place in the preheated oven for 20–25 minutes or until the vegetables are soft.

Tip everything carefully into a blender or food processor and whizz briefly to chop the nuts. Add the sherry vinegar and the coriander, and whizz again until blended, adding extra oil if necessary to make a thick sauce. Season to taste with salt and pepper.

Place the chops (or halloumi slices) on the barbecue and cook until done. The pork chops should take approx 3–4 minutes per side, depending on the thickness. Check by piercing the centre with a sharp knife; there should be no red or pink. The halloumi slices only take 2 minutes on each side. Serve with the Romesco sauce.

Aubergine soy sandwich with tattie scones and gooey cheese

SERVES 4

1 large aubergine

2 tablespoons soy sauce

4 tablespoons olive oil

2 garlic cloves, peeled and chopped

8 tattie (potato) scones

4 slices mozzarella (preferably buffalo)

watercress or rocket

EAST MEETS WEST takes on a whole new meaning here with Japanese soy sauce taking on the quintessentially Scottish tattie scone! The aubergines are marinated first to give them bags of flavour and then served hot with some mozzarella pressed between them. Do try to buy buffalo mozzarella for its delicate flavour. But, if not, ensure you buy balls of cows' milk mozzarella, not the long logs of tasteless factory-produced cheese. The aubergine and mozzarella is then sandwiched between two warm tattie scones and devoured hot and messy.

~

Slice the aubergine into eight thick rounds and place in a large, shallow dish.

Mix the soy sauce, olive oil and garlic together and pour over the aubergine slices. Leave to marinate for a couple of hours.

When your barbecue is ready, cook the aubergines for about 5 minutes on each side.

Towards the end of cooking, place the tattie scones on the grill and heat for a couple of minutes.

To serve, sandwich a slice of cheese between two aubergine slices and then place this on a tattie scone. Top with some watercress and then another scone. Devour while hot.

Tattie scones

Known most commonly as tattie scones, though sometimes as potato scones, these are flat girdle scones that are served for breakfast or tea. They are made by mashing potatoes with butter and then adding some flour while the potatoes are still warm. This mixture is then patted out to a thin round, cut into quarters and baked on a hot girdle. When freshly made, they are eaten warm with a thin smear of butter; leftovers can be toasted the next day. They are also good fried with bacon or spread with some butter and eaten with a bowl of broth or lentil soup.

Mustard mackerel

8 fresh plump mackerel fillets

about ½ small jar wholegrain mustard

MARTIN JOHNSON IS from the Out Skerries on Shetland. He now lives on the mainland of Shetland in Vidlin where the ferry comes in. He has fished since he was a wee boy and offered to take my husband Pat out one day when we were up in those most stunningly beautiful northern isles. Martin's wife Isabel and I had put in a request for lobsters for tea but they returned empty handed... Well, empty handed apart from six crabs in the creels and some fabulous mackerel! Martin barbecued some of the mackerel that night (having filleted them skilfully at sea) and the rest he smoked. We ate some with a horseradish-blitzed salad and others in a cream cheese and lemon paté. Divine.

— ∿ —

Place the fillets on a board and smear some mustard over the flesh side. Place them in your fish grill (four at a time, depending on the size of the grill) and then on to your barbecue, skin side down, for 4–5 minutes. Turn and continue to cook until done (about 10 minutes altogether). Serve with good brown bread and salad.

Barbecued Camembert

SERVES 8–10

1 × whole Camembert (about 300g / 10½ oz)

breadsticks, chunks of baguette or chicory leaves, to scoop

ANY CAMEMBERT-STYLE CHEESE is suitable for this recipe. Brie will also do but, because a whole Brie is larger in diameter than a Camembert, it is less easy to handle when the insides become gooey. Cooking times depend on the ripeness of your cheese and how hot your barbecue is. Start testing after about 3 minutes on the second side.

— ∿ —

Remove the cheese from its packaging and double wrap in foil. Place on a barbecue for about 5 minutes on each side. Test by gently pressing in the middle: it should feel soft and gooey. (You can always put it back on the heat again if it isn't quite ready, so don't be frightened to unwrap and test with an experimental breadstick.)

To serve, place on a plate and unwrap the foil. Eat like a fondue by dunking in breadsticks or hunks of baguette. (The skin or rind will break itself, so don't waste the lovely molten cheese by trying to cut it off.)

Burgers with the works

1kg / 2 lb 4 oz best minced beef
(preferably freshly minced steak)

1 small onion, peeled and very finely chopped

1 heaped tablespoon Dijon mustard

6 ciabatta (or burger) rolls, halved

mayonnaise, for spreading

6 pineapple rings or slices of beetroot

6 medium free-range eggs, fried (optional)

6 cos lettuce leaves

6 slices of tomato

tomato ketchup, for spreading (optional)

IN NEW ZEALAND, burgers are served with all sorts of amazing add-ons, including pineapple, beetroot and fried eggs. There are also some burgers served with grilled onion rings. They are large, tricky to handle and gloriously messy. Devour outside with plenty of napkins to hand!

Combine the minced beef, onion and mustard, and season generously with salt and pepper. Divide the mix into six and shape into burgers. Chill well.

Bring back to room temperature for half an hour before grilling on the barbecue for 5–6 minutes on each side until done (but still juicy).

To serve, spread mayonnaise on one half of a ciabatta roll and top with the burger, then a pineapple or beetroot slice (or both), a fried egg, lettuce and tomato. Spread some tomato ketchup on the other roll half, clamp on top of the burger and devour – messily – at once.

Puff candy
ice-cream

SERVES 6

4 heaped tablespoons granulated sugar

2 heaped tablespoons golden syrup

1 level teaspoon bicarbonate of soda

1 × 600ml tub double cream, lightly whipped

1 × 400g tin condensed milk

KNOWN AS HOKEY-POKEY in New Zealand, this is a delicious and incredibly easy ice-cream to make. First you must make the puff candy, which is also known as honeycomb because of all the little holes in it that make it similar to a honeycomb. It is great fun: and always seems like magic when the 'puff' element occurs!

The ice-cream itself is a doddle. The only tricky part is waiting for it to freeze before eating in large scoops, perhaps with a slosh of hot fudge sauce.

Butter the base and sides of an 18cm / 7 in shallow tin and line with baking parchment.

In a heavy-based pan, allow the sugar and syrup to dissolve slowly over a low heat, stirring well. Increase the heat to medium and bring to the boil, stirring constantly. Once you see bubbles, reduce the heat slightly and simmer for about 3 minutes, stirring again constantly until it is a rich golden brown. Do not allow it to become too dark, as it will have a slightly bitter flavour. (You are looking for the colour of a Crunchie bar.)

Remove from the heat, add the bicarbonate of soda and stir until it froths up. Tip immediately into the prepared tin. (It is really important to have buttered the base and sides or it will stick.) Leave to cool completely.

To remove, cut into large pieces or bash with the end of a rolling pin.

Combine the cream with the condensed milk in a large bowl and then stir in the broken pieces of puff candy. Turn into a large freezer container and freeze. (This does not need beating every hour, as some ices do.)

Chapter 18

Weekend Away

FUN AS IT is to invite a group of friends to stay, it is also good to go off to a rented house or croft together. Whether it's in the Hebrides, in Shetland or on the West Coast, the time away will not only be a chance to immerse yourself in Scotland's breathtaking scenery, but it will also be a time to enjoy rustling up something delicious in the kitchen. The burden of cooking away from home can be shared and each person – or couple – can bring their own ingredients or stock up in the local shops on the day that they are in charge of dinner. If you are on the coast, sea-food is an obvious choice. Even if there is no fish shop in town, you can often 'negotiate terms' with a local fisherman to buy some of his catch, whether a crab, lobster or some home-smoked haddock. If you are in the Highlands, game is a good option. If there is no butcher around, there are often farm shops and delis that sell venison or game birds from local estates. And if you are in the Hebrides or Shetland, lamb is my local preference, as there is surely no more apposite word than 'free-range' when you can see the sheep grazing over hills and glens and strolling along the seashore. And don't forget about the berries and soft fruits when they are in season; hopefully you might come across a nearby pick-your-own farm or village greengrocers selling local fruit.

Though you are with friends, there is bound to be at least one of your party who loves cooking so much that he or she brings an edge of friendly competitiveness to the proceedings. But whether you like to produce 'show-off', cheffy dishes or simple, homely ones, there will be a role for everyone – even those who hate cooking! Such a person could, perhaps, opt for washing-up or log-fire-cleaning duties, so they will be able to partake of the pleasures of the table as you all sit around at dinner, while looking out at a stunning sunset over a sea loch or a snow-capped mountain, with a clear conscience. And, when allocating duties, don't forget the all-important role of Person in Charge of the Wine!

Local seafood with show-off mayo

SERVES 6–8

Selection of mixed seafood, boiled
but not shelled – e.g. 2 crabs, 1 lobster,
1 bucketful of prawns or langoustines

FOR THE MAYO

2 medium free-range egg yolks

1 teaspoon Dijon mustard

1 teaspoon freshly squeezed lemon juice

approx 300ml / 10 fl oz oil
(½ sunflower, ½ olive)

a few drops of truffle oil (optional)

LAST SUMMER I stayed with my two friends Sue and Elisabeth in a remote croft overlooking Crobeag Bay on Lewis, in the middle of rolling hills dotted with sheep. We were deciding over breakfast what to eat that night and had opted for local seafood with mayonnaise. As I began talking excitedly about how I would use the eggs not needed at breakfast and the oil left over in a bottle bought for last night's vinaigrette to make home-made mayonnaise – while unconsciously acting out, with hands, spoon and bowl, how this would be done – they both stopped speaking and stared at me as if I was deranged. Elisabeth at last verbalised what they were both thinking: 'But why on earth would you want to do that, when we have a perfectly good jar of shop-bought mayonnaise already in the fridge?'

So, if making mayonnaise does not give you the thrill it does me (I must get out more), then a good shop-bought variety is fine. When my husband Pat and I stayed in Vidlin, north-east Shetland, in the house opposite, we covered the kitchen table with newspapers and spent the evening with friends, cracking crab claws and dunking into a jar of Hellman's zapped with a tiny splash of truffle oil.

The lovely thing about this dish is that you can shell the seafood at the table and dunk straight into the dish of mayonnaise casually and languorously. It is very messy indeed, so have plenty of napkins to hand…

———— ∼ ————

Place the yolks, mustard and lemon juice in a large bowl with plenty of salt and pepper. Whisk (or beat with a wooden spoon) for a few seconds. Very slowly dribble in the oil, literally drop by drop at first, whisking or beating constantly. Once an emulsion has begun to form, you can increase the dribble to a thin, slow stream.

Spoon the mayo into a bowl and add ½ tablespoon boiling water, to thin it down a little. Taste again and season with salt and pepper if needed – and some truffle oil if you like.

Serve in a bowl and dunk in your seafood.

Quick seafood pasta

SERVES 4

250g / 9 oz smoked salmon,
torn into small pieces

110g / 4 oz crab or lobster meat

1 × 300ml tub double cream

the juice and zest of 1 large lemon

300g / 10½ oz pasta (fettucine or tagliatelle)

2–3 tablespoons fresh herbs
(chopped dill/snipped chives)

2–3 tablespoons freshly grated Parmesan

THIS IS A dish I made one night in Shetland when we still had some boiled crabs left over from the night before. I found some locally smoked salmon, cream, a lemon and the best pasta I could buy and we were sorted. Serve with a salad and some good chilled white wine.

Put the smoked salmon, crab or lobster meat and double cream in a saucepan and add the grated lemon zest and plenty of freshly milled black pepper. Stir and leave aside at room temperature for at least half an hour.

Boil the pasta in plenty of boiling salted water until *al dente*.

Place the saucepan with the seafood mixture over a medium heat and cook until bubbling, stirring regularly. Remove from the heat and add most of the herbs and the Parmesan.

Drain the pasta and stir everything together. Add enough squeezed lemon juice to make the sauce a little sharp. Add more Parmesan, to taste.

Serve in warm bowls topped with the remaining herbs.

Slow-cooked lamb with chermoula

SERVES 6–8

1 large shoulder of lamb (about 2kg / 4 lb 8 oz)

3 large onions, peeled and sliced into rings

1 teaspoon sugar

FOR THE CHERMOULA

1 onion, peeled and chopped

6 garlic cloves, peeled and chopped

5 tablespoons freshly chopped coriander

3 tablespoons freshly chopped parsley

2 level tablespoons paprika

2 level tablespoons ground cumin

2 teaspoons cayenne pepper

the juice of 1 lemon

3 tablespoons olive oil

MAKE THE CHERMOULA paste at home and take it with you when you go away. You can then marinade the lamb overnight on the first night you are away in order to feast on it on your second night!

Put all the ingredients for the chermoula in a food processor with 1 teaspoon of salt and process until blended.

Place the lamb in a dish and prick all over with a sharp knife. Rub all over with the chermoula and then cover very loosely with foil. Refrigerate overnight.

On the day of cooking, preheat the oven to 150°C / 300°F / Gas 2.

Place the onion rings in the base of a roasting tin and sprinkle with ½ teaspoon of salt and 1 teaspoon of sugar. Toss the onions with your hands and then pour over 600ml / 1 pint of cold water. Place the lamb on top.

Roast in the oven for 4 hours, basting every hour.

Allow to rest for 10–15 minutes and then serve slices of the spiced lamb with spoonfuls of pan juices and the onions.

Venison Chilli

2 tablespoons vegetable oil

1 large onion, peeled and chopped

3 garlic cloves, peeled and chopped

1 red chilli, de-seeded and chopped

500g / 1 lb 2 oz venison mince

1 teaspoon freeze-dried oregano

½ teaspoon ground cumin

1–2 teaspoons chilli powder

150ml / 5 fl oz passata

1 × 420g tin kidney beans, drained

200ml / 7 fl oz dark beer (stout)

sour cream, to serve

THIS IS DELICIOUS served with baked potatoes.

~

Heat the oil in a large pan and gently fry the onion over a low heat until softened: this will take about 10 minutes.

Add the garlic and chilli, and fry gently for a further couple of minutes.

Increase the heat, add the mince, stirring well to break it up. Once browned all over, tip in the oregano, 1 teaspoon of salt, cumin and chilli powder. Stir and cook for 2 minutes.

Add the passata, beans and beer, stir well, and bring to the boil. Once boiling, reduce the heat to a low simmer, cover and cook for about 1½ hours.

Taste for seasoning and then serve piping hot with a spoonful of sour cream on top.

Raspberry cranachan cheesecake

SERVES 8-10

100g / 3½ oz oatcakes, crushed

75g / 2¾ oz digestive biscuits, crushed

40g / 1½ oz hazelnuts, toasted and chopped

75g / 2¾ oz butter, melted

900g / 2 lb cream cheese
(I use Philadelphia Light)

150g / 5½ oz golden caster sugar

2 tablespoons runny honey

1 rounded tablespoon plain flour, sifted

4 large free-range eggs

2 tablespoons whisky

1 × 150ml / 5 fl oz tub double cream

250g / 9 oz raspberries, puréed or crushed
with 1 tablespoon of icing sugar, plus extra
for serving

BRAMBLES (BLACKBERRIES) ARE also good in this luscious cheesecake, which can be made after breakfast one morning and left in the oven (switched off!) during the day. Then just take it out and put in the fridge once home.

⁓

Preheat the oven to 180°C / 350°F / Gas 4 and lightly butter a deep 24cm / 9½ in spring-form cake tin.

Combine the oatcakes, biscuits, nuts and butter in a bowl and then press into the base of the prepared tin and a little way up the sides. Bake for 10 minutes and then remove (leaving the oven on).

Meanwhile, place the cream cheese, sugar, honey, flour, eggs, whisky and cream in a food mixer and beat well until smooth. (Alternatively, place in a large bowl and mix using an electric beater.)

Once thoroughly combined, pour into the baked crust.

Spoon blobs of the crushed/puréed raspberry on to the top and then, using the tip of a sharp knife or a metal skewer, swirl the mixture all over.

Bake in the preheated oven for 15 minutes and then reduce the temperature to 150°C / 300°F / Gas 2 for a further hour until set round the edges but still wobbly in the middle.

Switch off the oven but leave the cheesecake inside for at least 2 hours – or overnight, if possible. Remove from the oven and allow to become completely cold before chilling, and serving with raspberries.

Cranachan

There are many different versions of this delicious pudding. It was traditionally eaten in rural Scotland at harvest time and the way they did it was to sit down at a table spread with bowls of cream, crowdie (traditional hand-skimmed cottage cheese), berries (raspberries, blaeberries, brambles), toasted oatmeal, heather honey and whisky, and each person would mix their own cranachan in their bowl, according to taste – so less whisky and more honey for the children.

Chapter 19

Hallowe'en Guisers Tea

IT USED TO be all about turnips, guising and treacle scones. Now it is pumpkins, trick or treating and devil's food cake. Yet another of our traditions to have been Americanised – in the States, Hallowe'en is big business. The shops are full of garish Hallowe'en tat for weeks and the magazines are packed with novel ideas about how to dress the kids in their ghoulish sartorial best, how to bake the most sublime pumpkin pie, and which variety of pumpkin makes the ideal lantern.

Pumpkin laterns have taken over from the humble turnip lantern here and, although it is far easier to hollow out a pumpkin, it is rather sad that the lowly turnip has been neglected. Now it only makes an appearance alongside haggis or in broth, instead of lighting the way for would-be Harry Potters through dark, eerie streets at nightfall. And so it seems our children have virtually forgotten all about guising – which involved days spent planning jokes, poems, songs and outfits – in favour of trick or treating, the modern day version.

Many of us in Scotland can still remember the thrill – after admiring the booty from a successful night's guising – of dooking for apples and grappling with dangling treacle scones. Large tubs (often baby baths) would be filled with the coldest water possible (were there no hot taps in the old days?) and crisp, shiny apples would be tipped in. They would then bob about until being lunged at by a child in ghostly attire, whose head was often ducked under the frigid water by naughty fellow guisers – usually a sibling. If make-up was likely to run, forks were permitted. And, although perching over the back of a chair above the apple tub with a fork in your mouth seemed like the soft option, I used to loathe the feel of the cold metal handle on my teeth and always missed the apple anyway, even after many attempts. True dooking – although wet as well as cold – is quick, if not painless.

And, finally, the treacle scones – the highlight of Hallowe'en for me. Thick wedges of doughy scones were tied through with string and then daubed with sticky, black treacle, before being suspended from a pulley or a clothesline. Hands would be tied behind backs and the spectres and bogles (ghosts) would attack the treacly scones with werewolf-like fervour until there were crumbs everywhere and – more memorably – faces daubed from ear to ear in sticky, black treacle.

Dead man's fingers with slime

SERVES 4–6

3 large baking potatoes

3 tablespoons olive oil

FOR THE SLIME

300g / 10½ oz frozen petits pois

15g / ½ oz fresh mint leaves

about 5 tablespoons extra virgin olive oil

POTATO WEDGES AND this lurid, green purée will be a favourite with everyone but, at Hallowe'en, it looks the part, too.

———— ～ ————

Preheat the oven to 200°C / 400°F / Gas 6.

Scrub the potatoes and then cut – unpeeled – into wedges. Place in a large plastic food bag and then pour in the oil. Season and shake well. Tip on to a solid roasting tray and roast for about 45–50 minutes, shaking or turning once, or until golden brown and tender. Drain on kitchen paper.

Meanwhile, boil the peas very briefly, until tender but still bright green. Tip into a sieve and hold under cold running water to arrest cooking. Pat thoroughly dry and then tip into a blender or food processor. Whizz with the mint and enough olive oil to form a sludgy consistency. Season to taste with salt and pepper, and serve with the potato wedges.

Hallowe'en Guisers Tea

Blood pies

MAKES APPROX 30–36

3 × small (300g) Stornoway black puddings

approx 500g / 1 lb 2 oz puff pastry

pesto sauce, for spreading

milk, for sealing

HERE IS AN alternative to sausage rolls that looks terrific for Hallowe'en: black and scary! But they also taste delicious...

— ∿ —

Preheat the oven to 200°C / 400°F / Gas 6 and lightly grease a baking tray.

Cut the puddings in half lengthways.

Roll out the pastry into three rectangles to fit two pudding halves, end to end.

Spread a line of pesto along the middle of each pastry rectangle and lay the puddings on top.

Dab some milk around the edges of the pastry and bring together, like sausage rolls. Place the rolls, join-side down, on the prepared baking tray. Brush the tops with more milk and bake in the preheated oven for about 20 minutes, or until golden brown and crispy.

Remove to a paper towel-lined board and leave until cold before cutting into small pieces. Reheat in the oven before serving.

Death by green chocolate

SERVES 10

250g / 9 oz plain flour

50g / 1¾ oz cocoa powder

1 teaspoon bicarbonate of soda

½ teaspoon baking powder

125ml / 4 fl oz extra virgin olive oil

150g / 5½ oz light muscovado sugar

1 teaspoon vanilla extract

3 large free-range eggs

300g / 10½ oz (about 1½ medium) courgettes, unpeeled, finely grated

100g / 3½ oz milk chocolate (minimum 30% cocoa solids), roughly chopped or bashed into chunks

ALSO KNOWN AS chocolate and courgette cake, this is delicious: richly flavoured, yet light and with flecks of green throughout, from the courgettes. The courgettes add a moistness – and a talking point! I like it just as it is, barely warm from the oven without any topping, but for Hallowe'en you could cover it with glacé icing and paint green spiders and a web on top. The recipe came originally from my New Zealand friend Pippa Lekner but I have fiddled with it to get it to where it is here.

Preheat the oven to 350°F / 180°C / Gas 4 and grease a 24cm / 9½ in spring-form cake tin.

Sift the plain flour, cocoa powder, bicarbonate of soda and baking powder into a large bowl with a pinch of salt. Remove one cupful and set aside.

Place the oil and sugar in a food processor and whizz until blended.

Add the vanilla extract and the eggs and whizz again. Tip this mixture into the bowl of dry ingredients and combine well.

Pat the courgettes dry and then toss them in the cupful of reserved dry ingredients and then add these to the bowl. Combine gently and then stir in the chocolate.

Tip this into the prepared cake tin, levelling the surface. Bake in the preheated oven for 30–40 minutes, or until a wooden cocktail stick inserted into the middle comes out clean.

Remove to a wire rack to cool before removing the sides.

Serve as it is or topped with glacé icing and decorated.

Irn-Bru cake

SERVES 10

300g / 10½ oz self-raising flour

¼ teaspoon bicarbonate of soda

280g / 10 oz golden caster sugar

200g / 7 oz butter

250ml / 9 fl oz Irn-Bru

100ml / 3½ fl oz milk

2 large free-range eggs

FOR THE FROSTING

150g / 5½ oz butter

50ml / 2 fl oz Irn-Bru

400g / 14 oz golden icing sugar

Irn-Bru

The iconic Scottish soft drink Irn-Bru is famous for its bright orange colour. It is advertised as having a slightly citrus flavour, but people have differing opinions as to its exact taste. It was first produced in 1901 in the town of Falkirk under the name Strachan's Brew. In 1946, a change in law required that the word 'brew' be removed from the name, as the drink is not technically brewed. The company therefore decided to change both halves of the name to a phonetic spelling, creating the current Irn-Bru brand. It has long been the most popular soft drink in Scotland, outselling all the other big names.

I BASED THIS divine recipe on my cola cake but here I use Scotland's national drink instead. I am pleased with the result as the distinctive flavour of Irn-Bru comes through subtly – not only in the cake but also in the frosting, which is an attractive pale orange colour. Kids will love this!

Preheat the oven to 180°C / 350°F / Gas 4 and butter a 24cm / 9½ in spring-form cake tin.

Sift the flour and bicarbonate of soda into a bowl and then stir in the caster sugar.

Meanwhile, slowly melt the butter in a saucepan over a low heat with the Irn-Bru. Once the butter has melted, pour this mixture slowly into the dry ingredients, stirring all the time.

Stir in the milk and eggs, and once everything is thoroughly (but gently) combined, tip the mixture into the prepared cake tin and bake for about 45 minutes, or until a skewer comes out clean. (Cover loosely with foil after 30 minutes if it is browning too much.) Leave on a wire rack for 10 minutes or so and then loosen and remove the sides. Continue to cool on its base on the rack.

To make the frosting, melt the butter in a saucepan over a low heat with the Irn-Bru.

Sift the icing sugar into a bowl and then pour the liquid over it, stirring or beating well until smooth. Pour over the cooled cake at once; since this is a soft icing it will slide alluringly down the sides, which is why it is easiest if you pour it soon after making.

Serve in slices to your ghouls and goblins.

Chapter 20

Hangover Breakfast

IN THE MIDST of the festive party season – or indeed any time of year when overindulgence has been the order of the day – there is a sure-fire way to soothe sore heads, and that is through food. Hangovers can only be assuaged by food – unless you are in a really bad state, in which case you should just go back to bed.

It's curious that after a night's bingeing, the body craves greasy, fried foods and stodge. A classic British fried breakfast fits the bill perfectly, so be sure to lay on bacon and eggs. You could also opt for another British classic – kedgeree – which can be made the night before and reheated in the morning, with melted butter drizzled in to keep it moist. Egg dishes are always welcome, whether scrambled with slivers of smoked salmon, or fried with a dash of truffle oil if your olfactory senses are up to it on thick wedges of buttered toast. The ultimate in comfort food.

What to drink with your food, though? If you cannot face any stimulant, such as coffee or tea, then hair-of-the-dog is worth considering. Many swear by a Bloody Mary with its super-healthy tomato juice. Worcestershire sauce and celery enhance the flavour, and Angostura bitters contributes to both flavour and health as it is prescribed for digestive disorders and queasiness. The vodka in a Bloody Mary has few medical properties but will add to the general levity.

And if frivolity is your aim, try this improbable-sounding brunch idea, from my friend Pippa in New Zealand. The day before (anticipating the hungover state), cut and remove a deep plug in a watermelon but ensure the base is still intact. Slowly pour in as much vodka as it will take. Replace the plug, seal with clingfilm and refrigerate for 24 hours. When you wake up the next day, tip any liquid that is not absorbed into a glass, slice up the boozy flesh (while sipping your melon vodka shot) and serve it at your merry brunch.

A flocculation of eggs

6 large organic eggs (the brightly coloured yolks
of organic eggs provide the best colour)

1 × 150ml / 5 fl oz tub double cream

50g / 1¾ oz butter, diced

IT WAS AT The Boatshed on Waiheke Island near Auckland that Chef Gordon McEwen asked if we would like a Flocculation. When this turned out to be the creamiest, silkiest scrambled eggs I had ever eaten, I requested them every day for breakfast. Scottish Chef Gordon told me he sometimes gets funny looks when he tells guests in the upmarket boutique hotel that he is about to flocculate. It is a term usually used for scientific purposes but he loves to use the word for its other meaning – to create his fluffy, light eggs. Its dictionary definition means 'to cause to form fluffy masses', in reference to clouds.

The cooking method is unusual, but follow it to the letter and you, too, will have the best, fluffy, light yet creamy scrambled eggs ever. Gordon serves his on home-baked ciabatta, which has been lightly toasted in a dry frying pan. I serve them in a slightly warm shallow bowl, with a thin slice of sourdough bread, fresh or toasted, on the side. Go flocculate…

But start cooking at least 15 minutes before you need to eat; this is not a dish to be hurried.

—— ∼ ——

Set a deep, medium-sized frying pan on to a low heat.

Meanwhile, lightly whisk the eggs and cream, and season with plenty of salt and pepper.

Place the butter in the pan. Once half melted, add the egg mixture and cook very gently for 10–15 minutes. During this time it needs constant attention: tilt the pan from side to side and move the eggs gently about (I prefer to use a wooden spatula), ensuring nothing sticks. You will see curds slowly begin to form. Once it is very soft and almost set, but still with a creamy, fluffy consistency, it is ready.

Spoon quickly into warm bowls and serve with sourdough toast or bread, buttered or plain. Eat slowly to enjoy every flocculated mouthful.

Hangover Breakfast

Kedgeree

SERVES 4

75g / 2¾ oz unsalted butter

10 green cardamom pods

1 teaspoon turmeric

1 teaspoon curry powder

1 medium onion, peeled and finely chopped

150ml / 5 fl oz single cream

a pinch of saffron stamens

450g / 1 lb undyed smoked haddock fillets,
cut into bite-size chunks

250g / 9 oz cooked basmati rice
(approx 125g / 4½ oz uncooked)

the juice of 1 large lemon

2 tablespoons freshly chopped coriander

3 large free-range eggs, hard-boiled and halved

THE CARDAMOM AND saffron in this dish give it a delightfully fragrant and exotic taste. It is important to cook the cardamom pods over a fairly high heat at first, until the pods 'crackle' slightly, to allow the flavour to infuse the butter. But then the heat should be reduced to medium for the rest of the cooking. Just like a biryani, the cardamom pods should not be eaten but rather pushed to the side of the plate – so warn your hungover guests!

~

Melt the butter over a low heat in a large, heavy-based saucepan.

Increase the heat to fairly high and add the cardamom pods. Fry briskly until they swell up and 'crackle' slightly (no more than 1 minute or they might burn), and then turn the heat down to low.

Add the turmeric and curry powder, stir well and then add the onion. Fry gently for 8–10 minutes, until softened.

Meanwhile, pour the cream into a small saucepan and place over a medium heat until hot. Remove from the heat and add the saffron. Stir, then allow to infuse for 10 minutes.

Increase the heat under the large saucepan to medium and add the fish. Cook for about 4–5 minutes, stirring carefully, until the fish is just cooked.

Add the cooked rice, stir well, and then pour in the saffron cream. Reduce the heat to low, stir well and cover. Cook for a further 4–5 minutes until everything is piping hot.

Season to taste with salt and pepper, stir in the lemon juice and coriander, and place the halves of egg on top. Remove from the heat and cover tightly. Allow to stand for 5–10 minutes, until the eggs are hot, and then serve.

Coconut milk porridge

1 cup pinhead oatmeal or porridge oats

1 cup coconut milk

blueberries, banana slices and
toasted coconut, to serve

THIS CAN BE made with pinhead oatmeal, if you
remember to soak it overnight. If not, use porridge
oats, as they require no soaking.

—— ∾ ——

Place the oatmeal in a saucepan with 2 cups of cold
water. (Leave to soak overnight if using pinhead. If
not, simply combine the porridge oats and water.)

Add the coconut milk and bring slowly to the boil
over a low heat and then add a good pinch of salt.
Cook until thickened (4–5 minutes) and then pour
into two porridge bowls.

Top with berries, banana and coconut flakes, and
serve with an optional jug of cold milk.

Porridge

To Dr Samuel Johnson's remark that oats were
a 'grain, which in England is generally given to
horses but in Scotland supports the people' came
the marvellous riposte by a certain Lord Elibank:
'And where will you get such men and such horses?'

A bowl of porridge is indeed the most healthy
and delicious breakfast possible. There are many
traditions associated with porridge in Scotland –
one being that porridge is referred to in the plural:
so you say, enjoy *them*! While medium oatmeal is
the most commonly used, my favourite grade is
pinhead with its pronounced nubbly texture. You
can use rolled or porridge oats, instead of proper
oatmeal, but they have far less flavour as they have
already been steamed or part-cooked. Oatmeal takes
at least 6–8 minutes to cook; with porridge oats,
however, you can reduce the cooking time by half.

On the now uninhabited island of St Kilda, it is
recorded that 'breakfast normally consisted of porridge and milk, with a puffin boiled in with the oats
to give flavour.' I am not sure how tasty this would
have been but, at a time when you had little else
but seabirds and oats to live on, needs must. Now
we can enjoy them with honey, coconut milk, berries and nuts – or just with salt, in the traditional
manner.

Bran and carrot muffins

MAKES 12

150g / 5½ oz self-raising flour

50g / 1¾ oz wholemeal self-raising flour

1 teaspoon baking powder

1 teaspoon ground cinnamon

75g / 2¾ oz butter, softened

75g / 2¾ oz light muscovado sugar

2 large free-range eggs

2 tablespoons black treacle

2 tablespoons natural yoghurt

150ml / 5 fl oz milk

75g / 2¾ oz bran

200g / 7 oz carrots (approx 2 medium),
peeled and grated

THESE ARE BASED on some of the wonderful muffins I ate during a trip to New Zealand. I had eaten terrific bran muffins in the States but the addition of carrots brought a whole new taste sensation; and, I like to think, a healthy one, too!

~

Preheat the oven to 190°C / 375°F / Gas 5 and prepare a muffin tin with twelve large muffin cases.

Sieve the flours, baking powder and cinnamon together in a bowl with ½ teaspoon of salt.

Cream the butter in a food mixer (or with an electric hand whisk), and then add the sugar and beat again until fluffy.

Break in the eggs, one at a time, and combine.

Pour in the treacle and yoghurt, and combine.

Reduce the speed to low, add the milk and the flour mixture and beat for 1 minute before adding the bran.

Finally, stir in the grated carrot.

Divide the mixture between the muffin cases and bake in the preheated oven for 20–25 minutes or until just done.

Serve warm.

Chapter 21
Gifts for Friends

WHETHER IT IS Christmas time or you just want to take a gift round to someone's house, I like to consider an edible home-made gift, instead of the usual box of bought chocolates or bottle of wine. The pleasure in giving something you have made – whether it's a cake, chutney, jam or sweets – is hard to beat. And you know that when the gift is opened and eaten, the recipients will think of you! Although the packaging is important, I admit gift-wrapping is not my forte so a neat bow or ribbon over cellophane usually does the trick. The main thing is that it is a gift from the heart – and from your kitchen.

Any of the tray bakes from Chapter 8 are also ideal as presents, or try one of the following suggestions.

Beetroot and ginger chutney

MAKES ABOUT 6–8 JARS

1.15kg / 2 lb 8 oz raw beetroot
(peeled weight), scrubbed

450g / 1 lb onions, peeled and chopped

450g / 1 lb cooking apples, peeled and chopped

450g / 1 lb raisins

900g / 2 lb golden granulated sugar

1.2 litres / 2 pints distilled malt vinegar

2–3 heaped tablespoons freshly grated root ginger

1 heaped tablespoon black peppercorns

TO STERILISE JAM jars, I put them through a full cycle in the dishwasher and dry them thoroughly. I then warm them in the microwave for a couple of minutes just before potting. Alternatively, they can be washed and then thoroughly dried in a low oven for 30 minutes.

— ∿ —

Grate the beetroot and place in a large preserving pan with the other ingredients and 1 teaspoon of salt. Stir well. Bring slowly to the boil over a medium heat, then reduce the heat slightly (you want something between a simmer and a fierce boil) and cook, uncovered, for about 1½ hours, stirring frequently, until thick.

Pot at once in sterilised jars. Either seal immediately or when completely cold.

Scottish tablet

MAKES ABOUT 40 PIECES

125g / 4½ oz unsalted butter

1kg / 2 lb 4 oz unrefined granulated sugar

300ml / 10 fl oz full-fat milk

200g / 7 oz condensed milk
(this is half a tin)

3 teaspoons pure vanilla extract

SCOTTISH TABLET IS thought of exceedingly fondly by most Scots; though never by their dentists. It is jaw-achingly sweet and not exactly healthy, but for a nation renowned for its sweet tooth, it is the national confection! I am certainly not alone in my memories of going to church fairs and garden fêtes with the primary purpose of buying tablet. Though there are many different flavours added to tablet these days, from ginger or cardamom to white chocolate and coconut, I prefer the traditional vanilla. But I only ever use pure vanilla extract – and plenty of it!

Butter a 23 × 33cm / 9 × 13 in Swiss roll tin.

Place the butter in a large, heavy-based saucepan (a reliable one) over a low heat and melt slowly.

Add the sugar and milk and a pinch of salt, and stir until the sugar has dissolved. Bring to the boil and simmer over a fairly high heat for 8–10 minutes, stirring often, getting into all the corners.

Add the condensed milk and vanilla extract, and simmer for 8–10 minutes over a medium/high heat, stirring constantly. If the phone rings, ignore it.

After 8 minutes, test for readiness (removing the pan from the heat as you test): it should be at the 'soft ball' stage, which means that when you drop a little of the mixture into a cup of very cold water it will form a soft ball that you can pick up between your fingers. On a sugar thermometer it should register 115°C / 240°F. If it isn't ready, put it back on the heat, stirring constantly, and test again after a further minute.

Once it has reached 'soft ball' stage, beat it with an electric beater (on medium) for 4–5 minutes (or by hand for 10 minutes), until it begins to stiffen a little and become ever so slightly grainy.

Pour into the prepared tin and leave to cool. Mark into tiny squares (remember it is rich!) when it is almost cold and when it is completely cold, remove the squares from the tin and store them in an airtight container or wrap in waxed paper.

Tablet

Almost unknown south of the border, tablet – a sort of fudge with a bite to it – is one of Scotland's oldest types of confectionery. There is a reference to it in Marion Lochhead's book, *The Scots Household in the Eighteenth Century*. She writes:

'Barley-sugar, tablet, crokain [from the French *croquant*, meaning crunchy] are all old and honourable Scots confections. Tablet might be made simply by boiling a pound of sugar in two gills of water until it candied; with cinnamon or ginger added for flavouring.' By 1929, when F. Marian McNeill wrote her book, *The Scots Kitchen*, milk had been added. Her recipe entitled 'Scots tablet' calls for granulated sugar, thin cream or milk and flavouring. For the latter, she suggests adding cinnamon, coconut, fig, ginger, lemon, orange, peppermint, walnut or vanilla.

Cupcakes

175g / 6 oz butter, softened

175g / 6 oz golden caster sugar

3 large free-range eggs

175g / 6 oz self-raising flour, sifted

½ teaspoon baking powder

FOR THE FROSTING

100g / 3½ oz butter, softened

100g / 3½ oz cream cheese
(I use Philadelphia Light)

2 teaspoons vanilla extract

250g / 9 oz icing sugar, sifted

chocolate buttons, undyed glacé cherries
or hundreds and thousands, to decorate

CUPCAKES ARE EXCEEDINGLY fashionable at the moment but only the name is new. We have been eating small cakes like this for years in Britain but we called them fairy cakes, angel cakes or simply buns. What has changed, though, is the icing. We only ever iced ours with a Presbyterian smear of glacé icing and a cherry. Now we have thick, gloopy icing piled so high it dominates the cake. It is too much, to my mind, but they are fun additions to the cake walk.

Variations to the frosting can be made by adding some citrus zest or ground cinnamon. For chocolate frosting, melt 200g / 7 oz dark chocolate with 200ml / 7 fl oz single cream, then cool before mixing with the frosting and chilling before icing the cakes.

Preheat the oven to 190°C / 375°F / Gas 5 and line a muffin tray with muffin cases.

Place the butter in a food mixer with the sugar, and beat for at least 5 minutes (or use an electric hand whisk) until the mixture is pale and almost white. There should be a noticeable difference in colour. Alternatively, place in a large bowl and beat well with a wooden spoon for 15–20 minutes.

Add the eggs one at a time, beating well after each addition. (Add a little of the flour if it looks a bit curdled.) Scrape well down the sides of the bowl.

Gently fold in the flour and the baking powder with a pinch of salt, and then divide the mixture between the muffin cases and bake in the preheated oven for about 20 minutes, or until springy and just firm to the touch. Remove the muffins from the tray (in their paper cases) to a wire rack and leave to cool.

Meanwhile, to make the frosting, place the butter, cream cheese and vanilla in a food mixer and beat until smooth (or use an electric hand whisk). Add the icing sugar, beat again till smooth. (Or, beat madly by hand until thick and smooth.) Top the cupcakes with the frosting and place in an airtight container.

Brazil nut rocky road

150g / 5½ oz Brazil nuts, halved

150g / 5½ oz marshmallows (a combination of pink and white looks best)

50g / 1¾ oz desiccated coconut

400g / 14 oz chocolate (I use ½ plain, ½ milk – aim for a minimum of 70% and 30% cocoa solids respectively)

OTHER NUTS, SUCH as hazelnuts or macadamias, are also suitable. And you could add natural (undyed) glacé cherries, if you like.

— ~ —

Line a 20–22cm / 8–8½ in square baking tin with baking parchment.

Combine the nuts, marshmallows and coconut and tip them into the prepared tin.

Melt the chocolate in the microwave, or break it into a bowl placed over a pan of boiling water and heat gently until it melts. Pour the liquid chocolate over the top, trying to cover the nuts, marshmallows and coconut evenly.

Chill until set and then cut into chunks.

Chapter 22
A Winter Party

MY UNCLE FRANK was turning ninety and our family wanted to celebrate. For Unc, as he is known to us, is a legend – a veteran of Tobruk in the Second World War and one of the founder members of the Carn Dearg Mountaineering Club in Dundee in 1949. So, the 'Oldies', as we label the family octogenarians, and the cousins and our partners sat down to a fabulous lunch at cousin Lynda's house in Dundee. There we were waited on by some members of the younger generation. Lynda's beef and porcini casserole was a huge hit, served with creamy dauphinoise potatoes and vegetables. The puddings included cloutie dumpling, my family's signature pud, served with lashings of custard and cream, of course (see page 200 for my cloutie dumpling recipe). More young then arrived – in the end there were some forty of us – ready to carry on partying well into the evening.

Having started lunch at noon, we – the older guests – got to bed after midnight, with the ninety-year-old birthday boy himself having left not long before. But it was the younger generation – the teenagers to twenty-year-olds – who partied on until about 4am... My daughter Faith got a text on Monday morning from a sympathetic friend: 'So how was the ninetieth? Boring?' 'The opposite,' replied Faith. 'Ninety is the new twenty-one!'

Goats' cheese stuffed tomatoes

SERVES 4

4 large or 6 medium tomatoes

150g / 5½ oz fresh goats' cheese (without rind)

1 dessertspoon Dijon mustard

1 garlic clove, peeled and crushed

1 medium free-range egg

freshly grated Parmesan, for sprinkling

olive oil, for drizzling

THESE ARE GOOD served with a couscous salad or by themselves as a starter. They're also perfect for a crowd: all you need to do is double or triple the recipe. They can be prepared in advance and chilled till ready to bake.

— ~ —

Preheat the oven to 190°C / 375°F / Gas 5.

Slice the top off the tomatoes and discard, then scoop out most of the insides, leaving a sturdy shell. Sprinkle the insides with salt and then turn upside down on kitchen paper. Leave for 10–15 minutes, by which time the paper will be soaked.

Using a fork, combine the goats' cheese, mustard, garlic and egg, and season with pepper.

Fill each tomato with some of this mixture and place them on a baking tray.

Sprinkle each tomato with Parmesan. Drizzle with oil and bake in the preheated oven for about 30 minutes until golden and bubbling.

Serve warm. Remember, these can be fully prepared in advance and refrigerated until time to bake.

Lynda's beef and porcini casserole

4 garlic cloves, peeled

4 stalks rosemary

50ml / 2 fl oz olive oil, plus extra for frying

350ml / 12 fl oz Port

1kg / 2 lb 4 oz braising steak, cubed

50g / 1¾ oz dried porcini mushrooms

250g / 9 oz pancetta, cubed

1 onion, peeled and chopped

2 large carrots, diced

2 stalks celery, diced

2 rounded tablespoons flour

350ml / 12 fl oz beef stock, hot

350g / 12 oz chestnut mushrooms,
wiped clean and thickly sliced

START THIS DELICIOUS dish the day before by marinating the beef.

~

In a large bowl, mix the garlic, rosemary and little black pepper with the oil and 50ml / 2 fl oz of the Port.

Toss in the steak, mix everything together well, and cover and marinade the beef overnight in the fridge.

The next day, preheat the oven to 150°C / 300°F / Gas 2 and soak the porcini in just enough hot water to cover them. Leave for 20 minutes or so.

Remove the beef and marinade from the fridge. Remove and discard the garlic; remove and retain the rosemary.

Heat a large casserole dish on the hob and add a splash of oil. Brown the beef in batches, then remove from the pan and add the pancetta and the vegetables. Cook for 10 minutes.

Sprinkle over the flour, cook for a couple more minutes, stirring.

Return the beef and rosemary to the pan with the stock, remaining Port, and the porcini mushrooms plus their liquid (about 150ml / 5 fl oz), and bring to the boil.

Season with salt and some more black pepper, cover and place in the preheated oven for 1 hour. Remove from the oven, add the chestnut mushrooms, stir and then cook for a further hour.

Check seasoning before serving with pappardelle pasta, mashed or dauphinoise potatoes and a green salad.

Ecclefechan tart with butterscotch yoghurt

SERVES 8

115g / 4 oz unsalted butter, softened

115g / 4 oz soft dark brown sugar

2 large free-range eggs, beaten

300g / 10½ oz raisins

the zest of 1 large unwaxed lemon

1 tablespoon lemon juice

100g / 3½ oz walnuts, chopped

½ teaspoon ground cinnamon

FOR THE PASTRY
50g / 1¾ oz golden caster sugar

75g / 2¾ oz ground almonds

150g / 5½ oz plain flour, sifted

115g / 4 oz butter, diced

1 large free-range egg

FOR THE BUTTERSCOTCH YOGHURT
1 × 500ml tub Greek yoghurt
(or full-fat crème fraîche)

4 tablespoons light or dark muscovado sugar

IN THE BORDERS of Scotland, there are many speciality tarts, all using dried fruits in some way or other. My mother's speciality was simply called Border Tart and is similar to Ecclefechan tart, which itself is not dissimilar to Pecan pie. Serve this warm with butterscotch yoghurt.

— ∼ —

Make the pastry in a food processor by whizzing the sugar, ground almonds, flour and butter together, and then adding the egg. Once amalgamated, combine with your hands (the pastry should be softish), wrap in clingfilm and chill well for a couple of hours.

Butter a deep 23cm / 9 in loose-bottomed flan tin and roll the pastry out to fit. Prick the base all over with a fork and chill again – for at least 3 hours, though preferably overnight.

Meanwhile, make the butterscotch yoghurt by spreading the yoghurt out in a shallow bowl and slowly sprinkling the sugar over the top. Leave this for at least 3 hours, though preferably 6–8, by which time there will be a sticky toffee goo on the top of the yoghurt. (The light sugar gives more of a butterscotch taste; the dark sugar more of a treacly one.)

Preheat the oven to 200°C / 400°F / Gas 6.

Line the chilled pastry case with foil and baking beans, and bake in the preheated oven for 10 minutes. Remove the foil and baking beans and continue to bake for a further 5 minutes. Remove from the oven and reduce the temperature to 190°C / 375°F / Gas 5.

Beat the butter and sugar together and then stir in the eggs, raisins, lemon zest, juice, nuts and cinnamon. Combine well and tip into the pastry case. Bake in the oven for 30 minutes, or until set, covering loosely with foil for the last 10 minutes to prevent the raisins burning.

Serve warm with the butterscotch yoghurt.

Border Tarts

Ecclefechan is a town to the south-west of the Borders and its tart is a fabulous affair – rich with dried fruit and nuts – and is based on the classic Border Tart. These days this constitutes a short-crust pastry case filled with a rich, spiced raisin filling but originally it was an enriched yeast pastry case filled with almonds, raisins, peel and marzipan, all bound together in an egg custard. The dough for the base would have been taken from the weekly bread-making.

There are similar tarts to be found all over the Borders, most notably Eyemouth tart, which is similar with its raisins and brown sugar in the filling, but also has coconut, walnuts and glacé cherries. Melrose tart is a ginger sponge baked in a pastry case.

Chapter 23

Chrîstmas Eve Drinks
for the Neighbours

EVERYONE IS BUSY on Chrîstmas Eve but, whether you have a house full
or just a quiet festive season planned, ît is a good time of year to invîte
the neighbours round for drinks. When you deliver their Chrîstmas
cards, wrîte a note about Chrîstmas Eve drinks, stîpulating not only a
start time but a leaving time, too! We have had some years of wondering how on earth we will not only tidy up the glasses but also manage to
sît down to family dinner before we need to start walking to churĉh for
the Chrîstmas Eve service. So 5 till 7pm works well – most preparation
ought to be nicely underway by 5pm and you will be more than ready
for festive ĉheer.

Here are a few recîpes for easy canapés – some hot, some cold – that
can be served throughout your party. Dish up cold ones first, then
bring on the hot ones; as for quantîties, always over-cater as ît's better
to have leftovers than to run out! And whether you proffer bubbly or
hot mulled wine, be sure to provide enough food to soak up the alcohol.
Right, whose turn is ît this year?

Warm lemon and mint olives

FEEDS A CROWD

4–5 tablespoons green olives
(best you can get; stone still in)

1 tablespoon extra virgin olive oil

1 fat garlic clove, peeled and crushed

the zest of 1 small lemon

1 tablespoon finely chopped fresh mint

DON'T FORGET TO provide another dish for the stones!

———— ∼ ————

Toss the olives with the oil and garlic, and then tip into a hot frying pan. Shake the pan about over a medium/low heat for 4–5 minutes until the olives are hot.

Remove from the heat, stir in the zest and mint, and tip everything into a bowl.

Eat warm – though they are also good at room temperature.

Mrs Thomson's cheesy oat biscuits

MAKES 30 BISCUITS

100g / 3½ oz butter, diced

100g / 3½ oz plain flour

100g / 3½ oz porridge oats

125g / 4½ oz mature Cheddar, grated

few shakes of cayenne pepper

MY COUSIN-IN-LAW SUE Hadden's mum, Joan Thomson, makes these fabulous little cheesy biscuits to serve with drinks.

— ∾ —

Rub the butter into the flour until it resembles breadcrumbs, and then add the oats, cheese and cayenne pepper. Knead into a ball, and then place on a long sheet of clingfilm. Once it is wrapped, roll out the dough (in the film) to make a long roll about 35cm / 14 in long. Chill for a couple of hours.

Preheat the oven to 180°C / 350°F / Gas 4 and lightly butter a baking tray.

Remove the dough from the fridge and take off the clingfilm. Using a serrated knife, cut into thin slices and place on the prepared baking tray. Prick the surface of each slice with a fork and then bake in the preheated oven for about 15 minutes, or until golden around the edges.

Leave on the baking tray for 10–15 minutes or so, and then remove the biscuits to a wire rack to cool.

Chicory with haggis and pomegranate

MAKES ENOUGH FOR 10–12

2 fat heads chicory, washed

½ haggis

pomegranate molasses, for drizzling

1 pomegranate, seeds removed

POMEGRANATE MOLASSES IS readily available in selected supermarkets and good delis.

——— ～ ———

First separate out the leaves of chicory and arrange on a platter.

Heat the haggis until it is piping hot (I do this in the microwave by cutting it open and scooping the contents into a microwave bowl, covering it with clingfilm and cooking for few minutes, stirring often), and then spoon some into each chicory 'boat'.

Drizzle generously with pomegranate molasses and then scatter over the seeds.

Serve while the haggis is still hot.

Crab tartlets with mango salsa

MAKES 24

24 tartlet cases (pastry cases or oatcakes)

1 mango, peeled, stoned and flesh finely diced

the juice and zest of ½ lime

¼ red onion, peeled and finely chopped

1 teaspoon red chilli flakes

2 teaspoons fish sauce (*nam pla*)

1 tablespoon freshly chopped coriander, plus extra coriander to garnish (optional)

125g / 4½ oz crème fraîche

approx 150g / 5½ oz fresh crabmeat (or hot-smoked salmon, flaked)

THESE ARE ALSO good with hot-smoked salmon instead of the crab. Only assemble these shortly before serving.

———— ~ ————

Set the tartlets out on a serving plate.

Make the mango salsa by combining the mango, lime juice, onion, chilli flakes, fish sauce and coriander. Set aside until ready to assemble.

Mix the lime zest with the crème fraîche and spoon some of this into each tartlet. Top with the crabmeat (or salmon).

Drain the salsa over a sieve to remove excess liquid and then spoon some on top of each crabmeat tartlet. Decorate with coriander leaves, if you wish.

Tapenade on toast

MAKES 24 TINY TOASTS

approx 150g / 5 oz black olives, stoned

2 fat garlic cloves, peeled and chopped

2 tablespoons capers

2 teaspoons anchovy paste
(or 1 teaspoon Patum Peperium)

4–5 tablespoons extra virgin olive oil

small rounds of toast, to serve

THIS VERY EASY and exceedingly tasty dish has its origins in Provence – and in the Scotland of a century ago! Monique Corbier and her husband Serge run a beautiful *chambres d'hôte* in Maussane, in one of my favourite areas of Provence, Les Alpilles. When she cooks dinner for guests, she invariably gives out little toasts spread with one of her fabulous olive spreads – green or black, the latter my favourite – when she serves aperitifs.

I have decided to use anchovy paste in this dish as it was used a lot in old Scottish cookery books – as well as anchovy essence. Lady Clark of Tillypronie, in her cookery book published in 1909, uses whole anchovies, anchovy essence and anchovy paste in dishes. And F. Marian McNeill, in her 1929 book *The Scots Kitchen*, advocates using anchovies and their essence in dishes including Partan Bree Soup.

Make this on the day of serving if possible; otherwise, I find the raw garlic taste becomes too strong.

———— ∾ ————

Whizz everything apart from the toasts together in a small food processor, until you have a purée (don't worry if it's a little chunky; that is good!). Don't add salt as the anchovy essence (and Patum Peperium in particular) is salty.

Spread on tiny rounds of toast and serve.

Crostini with smokie brandade, black pudding and salsa verde

MAKES 36–40

5–6 slices Stornoway black pudding, skin snipped off

36–40 crostini
(small rounds of bread toasted in the oven until golden)

FOR THE BRANDADE

1 Arbroath smokie (i.e. half a pair)

150ml / 5 fl oz milk

1 bay leaf

1 medium potato (about 200g / 7 oz unpeeled), peeled and boiled

1 garlic clove, peeled and crushed

2 tablespoons fresh flat-leaf parsley or lovage leaves

the juice of 1 lemon

2–3 tablespoons extra virgin olive oil

FOR THE SALSA VERDE

100g / 3½ oz fresh flat-leaf parsley

50g / 1¾ oz fresh mint

2 heaped tablespoons capers

1 heaped tablespoon Dijon mustard

2 fat garlic cloves, peeled and chopped

½ × 50g tin anchovies, drained and snipped

the juice of 1 large lemon

approx 6 tablespoons extra virgin olive oil

HEATING THE SMOKIE in milk and then leaving it to stand adds flavour since so much of the smokey flavour of the fish is in the skin and this infuses into the milk. The brandade and salsa verde can be made in advance but be sure to bring them to room temperature to serve. (You will have loads of salsa verde left over so either use it another day with roast fish or chicken, or freeze it in little ramekins. It is also delicious with the *Rib-eye Steaks and Roasted Mushrooms* on page 112.)

— ∼ —

Preheat the oven to 180°C / 350°F / Gas 4.

To make the brandade, place the fish in a saucepan with the milk and bay leaf. Bring slowly to the boil over a medium heat. Remove the pan from the heat the minute you see bubbles and cover. Leave to stand for 10–15 minutes.

Remove the fish from the saucepan. Flake the flesh, removing any bones or skin. Place in a food processor.

Add the well-drained potato, garlic, parsley or lovage, the lemon juice and the smokie-infused milk. Process briefly and then, with the machine running, add the oil – enough to give a soft, creamy consistency (like mashed potatoes). Check the seasoning (you probably will only need to add some pepper) and then turn into a bowl and cool to room temperature.

To make the salsa, remove the leaves from the herbs and place in a food processor.

Add the capers, mustard, garlic, anchovies and lemon juice, and whizz until blended. Pour in the oil – you may not need it all, just use enough to make a smooth, thick purée – and season to taste.

Lay the black pudding on a baking tray and place in the preheated oven for 10–15 minutes until cooked and crispy on the outside. Drain on kitchen paper and then cut into small pieces.

To assemble, spread each crostini with some brandade, top with a piece of black pudding then add a tiny dollop of salsa.

Arbroath smokie

The Arbroath smokie was first recorded historically in Arbroath Abbey's land register in 1178, as a gift from King William to the monks. Because the village where they were originally made – Auchmithie, three miles north of Arbroath – has been dated back to this time as a Pictish settlement, the origin of the humble smokie probably goes back a good deal further. It was only in the 1880s, when fishermen from Auchmithie were enticed to migrate to Arbroath and its new harbour, that the secret of their uniquely smoked haddock was taken with them.

A hot-smoked haddock, the smokie is made by gutting and beheading a haddock and then lightly brining and smoking it until just cooked (30–45 minutes). In Auchmithie – and later in Arbroath – smoke barrels were traditionally sunk into the garden, the rim being about a foot or so above the ground. Pairs of whole, headless, gutted haddock were salted, tied by the tails and hung on wooden poles over beech or oak chips, and then damp hessian bags were placed over the top. The fish would finally emerge a gorgeous bronzed, tarry colour with soft, succulent and delicately flavoured flesh.

Why did the tomato blush?
Because
it saw the **salad dressing**

...hat lies in a pram and wobbles?
A jelly-baby

Chapter 24

Christmas Lunch

WHY, WHEN IT occurs every single year, does everyone get in such a severe panic about cooking Christmas dinner? No matter what time you eat on the day, there is absolutely no reason to panic. (I have found Scots tend to eat later than down south – after 3pm, which is the perfect time to light the candles as it is getting dark outside.) It is just another roast dinner and, provided you are well organised and have as much as possible prepared in advance, then there is no reason why the cook cannot enjoy the day just as much as all the guests.

I tend to cook and freeze all the time during December. I often buy a good chicken and make some stock so that even the gravy can be made in advance and frozen. Red cabbage, bread sauce and cranberry sauce all freeze well, too. And potatoes and parsnips can be peeled and left in cold water overnight. The good thing about Christmas is that there are usually far more people milling around – so let them get stuck in and help. It's a family occasion after all!

Chestnut soup

SERVES 6

40g / 1½ oz butter

1 large onion, peeled and chopped

3–4 sticks celery, chopped

2 × 200g packets cooked chestnut pieces

1 litre / 1¾ pints hot chicken or turkey stock

1 large or 2 small sage leaves

squeeze of lemon juice

2 tablespoons dry sherry

crispy bacon pieces, to garnish (optional)

THIS RECIPE IS another that comes from my cousin-in-law Sue Hadden's mum, Joan Thomson, and is utterly wonderful – and I don't even like chestnuts!

Melt the butter in a saucepan over a medium heat and gently fry the onion and celery until softened; this should take about 10 minutes.

Add the chestnut pieces and stir well to coat.

Pour in the hot stock and season with plenty of salt and pepper and the sage. Bring to the boil, cover and reduce the temperature to simmer. Cook for about 20 minutes or until the vegetables are tender.

Remove and discard the sage and liquidise or purée with a squeeze of lemon juice and the sherry.

Check the seasoning and serve piping hot, with or without crispy bacon scattered on top.

Roast turkey

SERVES MANY!

1 turkey

butter, for lathering

FOR THE GRAVY

2 heaped tablespoons flour

1 litre/1¾ pints hot giblet stock

ROASTING TIMES

NB The final weight of the bird will include stuffing.

If the oven is set to 190°C / 375°F / Gas 5 and the foil tent method is used, allow:

40 minutes per 1kg / 2 lb 4 oz

(A 4.5 kg/10 lb bird will need 3 hours approx)

SINCE EVERY TURKEY is different in weight and quality, I have simply given guidelines. I would always recommend a free-range – preferably Bronze – turkey bought from a reputable butcher. Stuff the neck end with either the *Lemon Parmesan Stuffing* (see page 198), haggis or good sausage meat mixed with chopped cooked chestnuts.

～

Store your turkey in a cool place, preferably the bottom of your fridge. Remove the giblets and use them to make stock for the gravy.

It is often advised to fill only the neck cavity with stuffing (in which case, place a Bramley apple, peeled onion or halved lemon in the body cavity). But, provided you only half fill the body cavity, so there is room for air to circulate, there is little danger.

Sprinkle the bird with salt and pepper, lather with butter and place in a large roasting tin. Cover with a loose foil tent. (It must be loose, not tightly pressed down on to the bird.) Roast for the allotted time (see alongside), removing the foil about 30 minutes before cooking time is over.

To check the turkey is ready, it should have a lovely golden-brown colour all over. Take a fine skewer and pierce the thickest part of the thigh: if the juices run clear, it is ready; if they are pink, it is not yet done.

Leaving cooked meat to rest is important as it firms up the meat and settles the juices, which makes carving easier. Tip the juices from inside the bird into the roasting tin (to enrich your gravy), and then carefully lift the turkey on to a carving board and cover loosely with foil and a doubled tea towel. You can leave it for 20–45 minutes like this.

To make the gravy, spoon off the excess fat from the roasting tin, leaving only the dark juices – there should be about 2 tablespoons. Place the tin over a direct heat and add the flour. Stir well, scraping up all the bits, and then slowly add the hot giblet stock. Now change from wooden spoon to a balloon whisk: whisk for about 5 minutes until you have a smooth gravy. Taste for seasoning and continue to cook gently – whisking all the time – until hot and smooth.

Overnight bag of roasted veggies

vegetables, prepared and cut into large chunks

a good splosh olive oil

2–3 sprigs rosemary

2–3 sprigs thyme

THIS IS THE easiest way to roast vegetables as it can all be prepared the day before and then left overnight in the fridge. I use a mixture of the following vegetables: fennel, red onion, butternut squash and parsnips.

Place the prepared vegetables in a large (strong) plastic bag and add the oil, herbs and some black pepper. Seal tightly and toss madly about, and then leave somewhere cold overnight.

The next day, preheat the oven to 200°C/400°F/Gas 6 (or zap into the oven while the bird is resting).

Tip the veg into a large roasting tin and sprinkle over some sea salt. Roast in the preheated oven for about 45–60 minutes, shaking them about a couple of times, until golden brown and tender. They are fine warm as well as hot.

Perfect roast potatoes

SERVES MANY

potatoes, peeled and cut into large pieces

fat (½ olive oil, ½ butter is good; duck or goose fat is best), for roasting

ENSURE YOU USE a good sort of potato – I like King Edward, Vivaldi or Maris Piper; these will all give a nice crusty exterior and fluffy interior.

Preheat the oven to 200°C / 400°F / Gas 6.

Par-boil the potatoes in salted water for 5 minutes and then drain. Return to the pan over a low heat, cover and shake while the potatoes dry out to fluff up the edges.

Heat some fat – about 3 tablespoons, depending on the amount of potatoes – in a roasting tin by placing the tin over a direct heat. Once it is spitting hot, tip in your potatoes and coat them in the fat. Season well and roast in the preheated oven for about 45 minutes, basting a couple of times as they roast, until done.

Lemon and Parmesan stuffing

115g / 4 oz freshly grated Parmesan

55g / 2 oz fresh flat-leaf parsley

2 unwaxed lemons

150g / 5½ oz fresh breadcrumbs

2 medium free-range eggs

THIS WILL STUFF an average- to large-sized bird.

Place the Parmesan, parsley leaves, the grated zest of both lemons and the juice of one in a food processor. Add the breadcrumbs and eggs, and whizz until well combined.

Season with salt and pepper and stuff into the neck cavity of your turkey.

Mincemeat mile-high pie

SERVES 8

300g / 10½ oz ginger biscuits, crushed

115g / 4 oz butter, melted

400g / 14 oz best quality mincemeat

2 tablespoons whisky or brandy

1.2–1.5 litre / 2–2¾ pints quality vanilla ice-cream

a sprig holly, to decorate

THIS IS PERFECT for Christmas Day as you can make it a couple of weeks in advance then decorate it just before serving.

—— ~ ——

Mix the biscuit crumbs and melted butter together and press on to the base and up the sides of a 23cm / 9 in flan dish. Refrigerate for about an hour.

Heat the mincemeat in a saucepan over a medium heat for a couple of minutes (to melt the suet), and then stir in the whisky or brandy and allow to cool slightly.

Soften the ice-cream a little and then combine with the mincemeat. Spoon this mixture into the prepared flan dish, level the top and freeze until firm. (It takes up to an hour, depending on the quality of the ice-cream).

Serve decorated with a sprig of festive holly.

Cloutie dumpling

SERVES 12

450g / 1 lb self-raising flour, sifted

200g / 7 oz golden caster sugar

1 teaspoon ground cinnamon

1 teaspoon mixed spice

½ teaspoon bicarbonate of soda

125g / 4½ oz shredded suet

450g / 1 lb mixed dried fruit
(sultanas, currants and raisins)

2 level tablespoons black treacle

approx 450ml / 16 fl oz full-fat milk

flour and caster sugar, to sprinkle

IF YOU WANT to add coins, wrap five-pence pieces or charms in waxed or greaseproof paper and add to the uncooked mixture.

————— ∼ —————

Mix all the dry ingredients and the fruit and suet together in a bowl with a pinch of salt, and then drizzle over the treacle. Add just enough milk to make a soft dough of a stiff yet dropping consistency.

Dip a pudding cloth (or large tea-towel) into boiling water to scald and then drain well (I use rubber gloves to squeeze it dry). Lay the towel out flat on a board and sprinkle with flour and sugar (I use flour and sugar shakers): you want an even – but not thick – sprinkling. This forms the characteristic skin.

Now, put the cloth over a bowl, flour and sugared side facing up, and let it sink gently into the bowl (this helps the dumpling keep its shape). Spoon the mixture into the cloth, and then draw the corners of the cloth together and tie up securely with string, allowing a little room for expansion.

Take the cloutie from the bowl and place on a heatproof plate in the bottom of a large saucepan. Top with enough boiling water to just about cover the pudding (it must come at least three-quarters of the way up the side) and cover with a lid. Simmer gently over a low heat for about 3½ hours. Check the water level occasionally and top up if necessary. (You should hear the reassuring, gentle shuddering sound of the plate on the bottom of the pan for the entire duration of cooking.)

Preheat the oven to 180°C / 350°F / Gas 4 and place an ovenproof plate inside to warm.

Wearing rubber gloves, remove the pudding from the saucepan and dip briefly into a bowl of cold water (for no more than 10 seconds) so the skin does not stick to the cloth. Cut the string, untie the cloth and invert the dumpling on to the warmed ovenproof plate. Place in the oven for 10–15 minutes to dry off the skin: it should feel a little less sticky afterwards.

Remove from the oven, sprinkle with more caster sugar and serve hot with custard.

Cloutie dumpling

The word 'cloth' is the origin for this dumpling recipe. Cloot or clout is Scots for cloth and it refers to the cloth in which the dumpling is boiled. Unlike any other dumplings or steamed puddings, a characteristic 'skin' is formed, made by sprinkling flour and sugar into the cloth before filling with the mixture. The skin must be dried off before serving and this is done nowadays in the oven. But my mother's task (as youngest child) was to dry off the dumpling in front of the open fire-place. She would sit there on a stool for 15–20 minutes, turning the dumpling round and round until it was dried off and ready to eat. Since it was made only for special occasions, such as birthdays (in which case, there were silver threepennies hidden inside, similar to charms in a Christmas pudding), this was a chore worth doing well. It would then be eaten with custard, but is now also served with cream or ice-cream. The next day any leftovers would be served for breakfast: sliced and fried in rendered suet and eaten with bacon.

Chapter 25

Boxing Day Brunch

BOXING DAY IS a good day to have friends and family round for brunch. Having had a full-on feast the day before, the prospect of a thoroughly relaxed meal on the 26th holds great appeal. Also, since Christmas Day is usually very tiring, particularly for the cook, a brunch is a good idea since it can be any time of the day, from 11am to mid afternoon. A moveable feast!

And should the guests linger over the delicious food and coffee (or possibly the glass or two of bubbly), then suggest a brisk walk and everyone can come back for Boxing Day drinks and Christmas Day leftovers – even better!

I've given no puddings in this chapter as there are always so many cakes and desserts left over that if someone wants a sweet rush there will be plenty to hand.

Ham'n'haddie rarebit

SERVES 4

500g / 1 lb 2 oz undyed smoked haddock fillets

300ml / 10 fl oz milk

25g / 1 oz butter

25g / 1 oz plain flour

1 heaped tablespoon Dijon mustard

75g / 2¾ oz grated Cheddar

4 English muffins, split

4–8 rashers of Ayrshire bacon, grilled

HAM'N'HADDIE IS A traditional Scottish dish served at breakfast or tea. Ham means bacon in Scotland and so this most comforting of breakfast dishes is quite simply bacon (ham) with smoked haddock (haddie). It is traditionally made from Finnan haddock.

I have taken the traditional concept of ham'n'haddie and made it into a rarebit by mixing in some cheese and serving on muffins.

— ∼ —

Place the fish in a saucepan with the milk. Bring slowly to the boil over a medium heat, leave to bubble for 1 minute and then take off the heat and cover. Leave to infuse for half an hour or so and then strain over a sieve over a jug. Flake the fish and reserve the cooking liquid.

Melt the butter in a saucepan over a medium heat, add the flour and stir for a minute.

Pour the reserved fish liquor into the saucepan, whisking constantly, and cook over a medium/low heat until smooth.

Stir in the mustard, flakes of fish and grated cheese, and season to taste. Spread on top of the muffin halves and set on a grill tray.

Grill until the topping is gooey and hot, and then serve with a rasher of bacon on top.

Hot-smoked salmon potato gratin

SERVES 6

1.5kg / 3lb 5oz large potatoes

500g / 1 lb 2 oz hot-smoked salmon, flaked

1 × 600ml / 20 fl oz tub single cream

25g / 1 oz butter

2 tablespoons wholegrain mustard

25g / 1 oz fresh breadcrumbs

1 tablespoon olive oil

THIS RECIPE IS loosely based on a much-loved traditional Swedish recipe, Jansson's Temptation, which is a gratin of potatoes, anchovies and cream. I like to use hot-smoked salmon and add some wholegrain mustard to complement the fish perfectly. This is a meal in itself as it's so rich, but it's also great as part of a hot buffet.

Preheat the oven to 200°C / 400°F / Gas 6 and butter a large gratin dish.

Peel the potatoes and cut into very thin slices (I do this in my food processor). Place half the potatoes in the prepared gratin dish, seasoning with plenty of freshly milled pepper and only a little salt (the salmon is salty).

Scatter the salmon over the potatoes and then top with the rest of the potatoes and season again.

Place the cream and butter in a saucepan over a low heat and cook slowly until the butter just melts. Remove from the heat and stir in the mustard. Immediately pour this slowly over the dish, ensuring that all the potatoes are covered.

Cover the dish with buttered foil and cook in the preheated oven for 1 hour. Remove the foil, sprinkle over the breadcrumbs and drizzle with the oil. Return to the oven for a further 40 minutes or so, or until the potatoes are completely soft.

Allow to rest for at least 10 minutes before serving.

Turkey and mango quesadillas

SERVES 6

6 large soft flour tortillas

3 teaspoons Dijon mustard

150g / 5½ oz mature Cheddar, grated

150g / 5½ oz cooked turkey, chopped

1 mango, peeled, stoned and diced

4–5 spring onions, chopped

2 tablespoons freshly chopped coriander

FOR ANY GUESTS who like spicy food, offer a tangy chilli salsa to go with this.

———— ∼ ————

Preheat the oven to 200°C / 400°F / Gas 6 and oil a baking tray.

Lay the tortillas on to a board and spread ½ teaspoon of mustard around the edges of each one: this will help to seal them.

Divide the cheese into six and spread over one half of each tortilla.

Mix together the remaining ingredients and season well. Divide this between the six tortillas, piling it on top of the cheese. Fold the tortilla in half to close it over the top of the turkey and seal the edges by pressing down firmly with your thumbs. Place the quesadillas on the prepared baking tray and bake in the preheated oven for 8–10 minutes, until the cheese has melted and the top is tinged with golden brown. Eat at once.

Hebridean fishcakes

SERVES 4

1 large potato (weighing about 325g / 11½ oz unpeeled), peeled and cut into chunks

40g / 1½ oz butter

approx 325g / 11½ oz hot-smoked salmon

the juice of 1 small lemon

2 tablespoons finely chopped fresh dill

1 small free-range egg, beaten

1 heaped tablespoon flour

4 heaped tablespoons medium oatmeal

olive or rapeseed oil, for frying

THESE ARE BASED on a recipe given to me by Rhona Anderson, cook at the Claddach Kirkibost Centre Café on North Uist. Rhona uses both freshly poached salmon and the South Uist hot-smoked salmon from Salar Smokehouse, but I like the full smokey flavour so use all smoked. I also like to coat them in medium oatmeal, but you can use breadcrumbs instead. Serve them with a little salad of tomatoes and avocado, dressed in lemon juice and olive oil, or – as Rhona does in the café – with home-made spicy tomato chutney. They can be prepared in advance, frozen and then thawed before cooking. You can double up quantities, if necessary, for a crowd.

— ∿ —

Boil the potato until tender and then drain thoroughly. Mash with the butter and season with plenty of salt and pepper, to taste.

Flake the salmon into large chunks and combine gently with the potatoes, adding the lemon juice and dill. Check the seasoning.

Form this mixture into four fishcakes and chill for at least an hour.

Set three plates out in a row. Put the egg in one, the flour in another and the oatmeal in the third. Dip each fish cake first into the egg, then the flour and finally the oatmeal. You can refrigerate the fishcakes again (or freeze them) at this point if you are making them in advance.

Preheat the oven to 180°C / 350°F / Gas 4.

Heat some oil in a small frying pan over a high heat and, once hot, fry the fish cakes for 2 minutes on each side, until golden. Place on to a baking tray and cook in the preheated oven for about 20 minutes, or until heated through.

Boxing Day Brunch

Useful Addresses

ARBROATH SMOKIES
R. R. Spink and Sons
Kirkton Industrial Estate
Arbroath DD11 3RD
Tel 01241 872023

ASPARAGUS
A.H & H.A Pattullo
Eassie Farm
by Glamis
Tayside DD8 1SG
Tel 01307 840303

AYRSHIRE BACON
Ramsay of Carluke
22 Mount Stewart Street
Carluke ML8 5ED
Tel 01555 772277
www.ramsayofcarluke.co.uk

BEEF
Donald Russell
Harlaw Road
Inverurie
Aberdeenshire AB51 4FR
Tel 01467 629666
www.donaldrusselldirect.com

BLACK PUDDING AND HEBRIDEAN LAMB
Stornoway black pudding
Charles Macleod Butchers
Ropewood Park
Stornoway HS1 2LB
Tel 01851 702445
www.charlesmacleod.co.uk

BREAD, OLIVE OIL, HERBS AND MORE
Valvona & Crolla Ltd
19 Elm Row
Edinburgh EH7 4AA
Tel 0131 5566066
www.valvonacrolla.com

FARMHOUSE CHEESE
Iain J. Mellis Cheesemonger
30a Victoria Street
Edinburgh EH1 2JW
Tel 0131 2266215
&
492 Great Western Road
Glasgow G12 8EW
Tel 0141 3398998
www.mellischeese.co.uk

HAGGIS AND BLACK PUDDING
Macsween of Edinburgh
Bilston Glen
Loanhead EH20 9LZ
Tel 0131 4402555
www.macsween.co.uk

HAGGIS, SHETLAND LAMB, SAUSAGES
Crombie's of Edinburgh
97 Broughton Street
Edinburgh EH1 3RZ
Tel 0131 5570111
www.sausages.co.uk

HERBS
Scotherbs
Kingswell
Longforgan
near Dundee DD2 5HJ
Tel 01382 360642
www.scotherbs.co.uk

MALT WHISKIES
Royal Mile Whiskies
379 High Street
Edinburgh EH1 1PW
Tel 0131 6226255
www.royalmilewhiskies.com

OATMEAL

The Oatmeal of Alford
Montgarrie Mill
Alford
Aberdeenshire AB33 8AP
Tel 01975 562209
www.oatmealofalford.com

Hamlyns of Scotland
Grampian Oats
Boyndie
Banff AB45 2LR
Tel 01261 843330
www.hamlynsoats.co.uk

OYSTERS

Islay Oysters
Craigens
Gruinart
Isle of Islay
Tel 01496 850256

Loch Fyne Smokehouse
Ardkinglas
Argyll
Tel 01499 600217
www.lochfyne.com

POTATOES

Knowes Farm Shop
By East Linton
East Lothian EH42 1XJ
Tel 01620 860010

SCOTCH PIES AND SAUSAGES

Stuart's of Buckhaven
19 Randolph Street
Buckhaven
Fife KY8 1AT
Tel 01592 713413

SMOKED GAME

Rannoch Smokery
Kinloch Rannoch
By Pitlochry
Perthshire PH16 5QD
Tel 0870 1601559
www.rannochsmokery.co.uk

SMOKED AND FRESH FISH,
SHELLFISH

George Armstrong
80 Raeburn Place
Edinburgh EH4 1HH
Tel 0131 315 2033
www.armstrongs
ofstockbridge.com

SMOKED SALMON

Grieg Seafood Hjaltland
Lerwick
Shetland
www.shetland-products.com

Hebriden Smokehouse
North Uist
www.hebrideansmokehouse.com

Hot-smoked salmon:
Salar Smokehouse, South Uist
www.salar.co.uk

SOFT FRUITS

G & G Sinclair
West Craigie Farm
South Queensferry EH30 9TR
Tel 0131 3191048
www.craigies.co.uk

(FARMED) VENISON

Fletchers Fine Foods
Reediehill Farm
Auchtermuchty KY14 7HS
Tel 01337 828369
www.seriouslygoodvenison.co.uk

WILD GAME

Highland Game
Baird Avenue
Dryburgh Industrial Estate
Dundee DD2 3TN
Tel 01382 827088
www.highlandgame.com

Useful Addresses

Index

Index

213